THE GREAT BOOK OF SOCCER

Interesting Facts and Sports Stories

Sports Trivia Vol.5

Bill O'Neill

ISBN-13:978-1985155800

DON'T FORGET YOUR
FREE BOOKS

GET THEM FOR FREE ON WWW.TRIVIABILL.COM

CONTENTS

Introduction 1

CHAPTER 1: Soccer's Evolution 2

    Ancient Times 2

    Britain Starts the Development Process 3

    Football Association Founder Members 4

    The First Soccer Cup 5

    International Soccer 6

    The Issue of Professionalism 7

    League Soccer in England 8

    Soccer Further Afield 9

    FIFA 10

    The First World War 11

    Peace Is Restored 13

    The World Cup Begins 14

    The History of Club Soccer 16

    The Arsenal Side of the 1930s 18

    World War II 19

Facts & Figures 21

Trivia Questions 24

    Answers 26

CHAPTER 2: A Changing World 27

Soccer Starts Again 27

A New World..27

FIFA Starts to Grow 28

Great Britain v The Rest of Europe 28

Stanley Matthews' Cup Final 30

Hungary 31

Germany Opens its Account..32

A Teenager in Sweden 34

The Munich Air Disaster..35

Real Madrid 36

Tottenham's "Double" 37

UEFA 39

Africa 41

North America..42

A Rivalry Is Born 42

The Asian Cup..43

Facts & Figures 44

Trivia Questions 48

Answers 50

CHAPTER 3: Two Decades of Classic Soccer..51

European Cup Winners Cup 51

Benfica..52

The Milan Giants 53

North Korea 54

The Cup Comes Home? 55

Celtic 56

A Night at Wembley 57

The Arsenal Double 58

Bob Stokoe and Sunderland 58

South America 60

Ajax 61

Dutch Frustration 62

Bayern Munich 63

Liverpool 63

Kevin Keegan 64

Facts & Figures 66

Trivia Questions 70

Answers 72

CHAPTER 4: Change, Controversy and Disaster 73

First Million Pound Player 73

Brian Clough and Nottingham Forest 74

Aston Villa 75

Aberdeen 77

Michel Platini 78

Liverpool and Heysel 79

Maradona 80

The Hand of God 81

African Awakening 83

Russia Hides the Truth? 84

Asia 85

Marco van Basten 85

North American Soccer League 86

Hillsborough 87

Gazza and 1990 87

Facts & Figures 89

Trivia Questions 93

Answers 95

CHAPTER 5: A Truly Global Game 96

The Formation of the Premier League 96

Denmark Springs a Surprise 98

The Bosman Ruling and its Implications 99

The USA Hosts the World Cup 100

A French First 101

Japan & South Korea 102

Sir Alex Ferguson 104

The Class of '92 105

George Weah 107

Real Madrid Is Back 108

Women's World Cup.. 109

The Demise of the European Cup Winners' Cup 110

The Expansion of the Champions League 111

The Inaugural World Club Championship 113

The Invincibles.. 114

Facts & Figures 116

Trivia Questions 120

Answers 122

CHAPTER 6: High Finance & A Power Struggle 123

Abramovich and Chelsea 123

One Night in Istanbul 124

Manchester City 125

South Africa 127

Spain 128

PSG & Qatar 129

Lionel Messi... 130

Barcelona... 131

FIFA Scandals... 132

Russia & Qatar... 133

Cristiano Ronaldo 135

Real Madrid Again... 135

The Growth in Premiership Revenue 137

Fair Play 138

What the Future Holds 140

Facts & Figures 144

Trivia Questions 148

Answers 150

MORE BOOKS BY BILL O'NEILL... 152

INTRODUCTION

Soccer is the most popular game in the world. Its governing body, FIFA, claims that over 240 million people play the game, and there is no doubt that the major games attract huge audiences worldwide. FIFA has always aimed to make soccer a genuinely worldwide sport, and in that aim, it has succeeded.

Soccer had humble and slightly confusing beginnings, and its appeal to the masses in Europe where soccer developed was and is without question. The many stories that soccer has produced over a century and a half make interesting reading, and hopefully as a soccer fan, you will enjoy reading about those within this book. You may know some of them, while others will be new.

What to include in the book and what to omit is inevitably subjective, but it should give readers the incentive to investigate specific stories and specific periods of history in greater depth.

The book is laid out in six chapters, broadly in chronological order. Each chapter has fifteen stories followed by twenty facts and figures and five trivia questions about the chapter itself. You can ask your friends some questions when you are waiting for kick off or it is halftime.

CHAPTER 1
SOCCER'S EVOLUTION

Soccer wasn't always the multi-million-dollar game that it is today. Even just a couple of decades ago, soccer had yet to make the impact that it does now. Satellite television and the internet have been the catalyst for supporters to be able to watch their favorites in whichever time zone they are living. The giants of the game, clubs from Europe primarily, now regularly reinforce the support they receive worldwide by traveling to play friendly matches far and wide in front of capacity crowds. In itself, that is a world away from the game's beginnings.

Ancient Times

Soccer is a simple game; it just needs an open space and something round that will roll. Balls in very early times—and there is evidence that a form of soccer was played by the Ancient Greeks and Egyptians as well as the Chinese—were very basic, and the object of early ball games was often just to retain the ball as long as possible. The form of soccer that was closest to the game we know today was in China where mention is made of the use of feet; elsewhere the game often involved a stick. Tsu'Chu, (meaning "kicking the ball") as it was known, was thought to be a form of military training during the Han Dynasty (206 B.C.–220 A.D.). The ball was small and leather, but the goals were 30 feet high. Over the years, other parts of the world played a form of soccer—the American Indian, the Maoris of New Zealand, the Australian Aborigines, and the Japanese.

Britain Starts the Development Process

It took longer for the game to evolve in Europe, but once it did, it was that continent that gave the game momentum. Ancient ball games played in Britain in medieval times sometimes involved using the whole village as the "pitch" with a pig's bladder used as the ball. Each team sought to get it through the opposition goal, often at the far end of the village. There weren't many goals scored in medieval Britain! There were also minimal rules, so it was very much a game where everyone could "let off steam". It had a potential for violence and was banned in some places as a nuisance. It was as the Industrial Revolution approached that this form of the game began to fade. There were fewer open spaces as industry developed, and less free time. There were similar developments elsewhere in Europe, notably Germany, France, and Italy.

The commonly held thought is that it was the public schools of England that put some form to the game. Pitches with bar less goals at each end and the concept of goalkeepers were introduced, but there were still some games that permitted the use of hands. The sports of soccer and rugby diverged, with schools in the 19th Century gradually developing the game as we know it today. Inter-school competition provided the incentive to form a proper set of rules.

A fairly recent find, 2011, actually attributes the origin of soccer to Scotland. Italy had always claimed the honor, but mention of a game played in Scotland seems to indicate the Scots are the initiators of soccer as we now know it. A game of soccer is described in a book called "Vocabula" written by a man from Aberdeen in the 14th Century! That is not the only evidence. A leather soccer ball dated as 15th Century was found behind a wall in Stirling Castle. There was a club founded in Edinburgh in 1824, but it only survived for 17 years, so it no longer existed when the first real set of rules was prepared.

In 1848, the "Cambridge Rules" were devised by the University, but there was still an element permitting the use of hands until the Football Association was formed in 1863, essentially by schools within the Greater London Area. The use of hands was forbidden, which resulted in some sides deciding against joining the Association.

Football Association Founder Members

The clubs who met on the evening of 26th October 1863 at the Freemasons' Tavern in Great Queen Street in Holborn were:

Barnes, Blackheath Proprietory School, Charterhouse, War

Office (subsequently Civil Service that celebrated its 150th Anniversary in 2013), Blackheath, Kensington School, Crusaders, Forest (Leytonstone), No Names (Kilburn), Crystal Palace (though no connection with the present-day club), Surbiton, and Perceval House (Blackheath).

It took six meetings to finally agree on the set of rules which was made available in a published pamphlet for the price of 1 shilling and sixpence (7p or 10 cents US today). The FA was very keen to get a game played under the agreed rules, and that took place on 18th December 1863, between Barnes and Richmond on Limes Field in Barnes on the south bank of the River Thames. The game finished goalless.

There was no way in which such a small organization could have a huge impact on national sport, but it was a start, and within 25 years there were 128 members and organized leagues, but plenty happened in the intervening years.

The First Soccer Cup

One decision that did have a lasting impact on soccer was the decision to run a cup competition. The FA Cup is the oldest soccer competition in the world and remains an important part of English soccer to this day.

A short announcement in 1871, "That it is desirable that a Challenge Cup should be established in connection with the Association for which all clubs belonging to the Association should be invited to compete" was historic. The initiator was Charles Alcock, the 29-year-old secretary of the FA who had just taken the post the year before. He had attended Harrow School and played in an inter-house knockout competition and suggested it would be ideally suited for the FA.

By that time, there were 50 members of the FA, but only 15 decided to enter. With the exception of Donnington Grammar School in Lincolnshire and Queen's Park in Glasgow, all the entrants were from the South East. It did not go especially well, with many clubs withdrawing and others therefore receiving byes. In total, only 12 teams played, and only 12 matches had taken place before the finalists met at Kennington Oval when Wanderers beat Royal Engineers 1 − 0. The attendance incidentally was approximately 2,000, everyone paying a shilling to watch.

Years later, in 1923, when Bolton beat West Ham in the first Final played at Wembley, demand was staggering with real danger of very serious injuries as so many people tried to get in. In the event, there were many injuries. The ground was designed to hold 125,000, but many more got in, and the kick-off was delayed to avoid utter chaos. Subsequent Finals became all-ticket as a result.

International Soccer

Charles Alcock was a man full of ideas. He wrote to the Glasgow Herald in November 1870 and announced an international between England and Scotland. It took place at Kennington Oval on 19th November, though it was a fairly artificial affair because all the Scottish team lived in London. England won 1 – 0.

Queen's Park in Glasgow existed, but the Scottish FA was yet to form, so the first game between the countries was organized by Queen's Park and played at the ground of West of Scotland Cricket Club a year later, 30th November 1872. The crowd was 4,000 and the entrance fee that same shilling. Everyone agreed what an enjoyable day it was, played in good spirit, even though neither side could manage to score.

The Issue of Professionalism

The fact that spectators were charged for getting into games inevitably led to the question of the payment of players. The FA had been founded on the basis that players were strictly amateur, but obviously talented players had to earn a living which meant having a full-time job as well as training and playing. Decades later, it was still common that good players worked a shift in a mine, shipyard, or heavy engineering company before playing for their teams.

The pressure for payment grew through the 1870s due to the popularity of the game and the revenue being generated.

It is important to try to cast your mind back to what life was like in the later decades of the 19th Century. Road and rail travel was not quick even though there was nowhere near the volume of travelers moving around in those days. The FA was based in London, so it was important that county and district associations played a part in the development of soccer. From the mid-1870s over the next ten years, a host of new clubs were competing in their own regions, and inevitably the debate on the game and its structure raged throughout the country. Professionalism was acceptable, but it is important to realize that the "compensation" that players received was fairly insignificant and certainly not a substitute for a full-time wage.

It was in 1888 that leagues were formed for the first time, though they were yet to be national.

League Soccer in England

There were just twelve teams in the first football league competition that ran through the winter of 1888/9. Only one of them does not exist today, Accrington, which ceased to exist in 1896, although Accrington is a Lancashire town with a football league club today. The Clubs that have the honor of being founder members of the Football League in alphabetical order are Accrington (folded 1896), Aston Villa, Blackburn, Bolton, Burnley, Derby, Everton, Notts County, Preston North End, Stoke, West Bromwich Albion, and Wolverhampton Wanderers.

A year later, a parallel competition was formed calling itself the Football Alliance. That also had twelve clubs which were Ardwick (Man City), Birmingham St. George (Disbanded 1892), Bootle (Left), Burton Swifts (Folded 1910), Crewe Alexandra, Darwen,

Grimsby Town, Lincoln City, Long Eaton Rangers, Newton Heath (Man United), Nottingham Forest, The Wednesday (Sheffield Wednesday), Small Heath (Birmingham City), Stoke, Sunderland Albion (Disbanded), and Walsall Town Swifts (Walsall FC).

After three seasons, the twenty-four clubs merged to run two divisions of twelve clubs.

The oldest of these twenty-four teams is Notts County that was formed in 1862, a year before Aston Villa, which has seven league titles to its name. Six of those titles were prior to the First World War with Sunderland a close second with five successes. Historically, Everton is the most successful of these clubs with nine titles, although Walton Heath was later to become Manchester United that has more league titles than any other club to date.

Incidentally, the winner of the first League Championship was Preston North End that went through the 22-game season undefeated. The Wednesday was the first Alliance Champion, with Stoke and Nottingham Forest winning in the following years before the Alliance disbanded, with its clubs effectively becoming the Football League's Second Division.

Soccer Further Afield

The game was clearly not exclusively British. Other countries were not slow in organizing soccer in their own lands. The Netherlands and Denmark were both just a year behind the first

English league, with Argentina starting in 1893 and Chile two years later.

That same year, Switzerland and Belgium started league competition, quickly followed by Italy (1898), Germany and Uruguay (both 1900), Hungary (1901), France (1903), and Finland (1907).

The game was being played elsewhere, of course, without there being defined competitions.

FIFA

The governing body that still oversees the world game was formed in 1904 with just seven members, all European, but not including England or Germany, though the latter announced that it would join as soon as the body was announced. The seven founders of the La Federation Internationale de Football Association (FIFA) were Belgium, Denmark, France, the Netherlands, Spain, Sweden, and Switzerland.

England had prevaricated over an international body, so the Secretary of French football, Robert Guerin, took the initiative and contacted other national associations. Belgium and France met in an international game in 1904, and with England clearly not interested, FIFA was formed with each national association paying an annual fee and recognizing a defined set of rules.

England joined a year later, quickly followed by the other "Home Countries", Scotland, Wales, and Ireland as well as

Austria, Italy, and Hungary. There was the first attempt at an international competition in Switzerland, but it was not a success. But there was certainly progress in creating a uniform set of "Laws of the Game."

There was success in arranging an international competition as part of the Olympic Games of 1908 in England and again in Stockholm four years later, but the issue of professionalism and the amateur ethos of the Olympic movement clouded the competitions which were both won by England.

Between these two competitions, FIFA was able to spread its membership beyond Europe. South Africa joined in 1909, Chile in 1912, while the USA joined a year later. The first World War meant that all talks on football were small-scale, and proper competition almost non-existent.

The First World War

Britain declared war on Germany in August 1914, and although some sports, primarily amateur, stopped immediately, the Football League started the 1914/5 season with many footballers contracted to clubs and unable to enlist without those clubs approving their release from the contracts. In less than a month, 50,000 had enlisted to fight, some up to 35 years old, but footballers were not among them. Pressure increased as the first casualties were announced.

England's centre-half, Frank Buckley, joined the Football

Battalion within the Middlesex Regiment in December and was given the rank of lieutenant because of his previous army experience. The Battalion soon had a full complement of 600, but few were footballers. In the end, the Football League bowed to pressure to get the clubs to release unmarried players from their contracts.

In Scotland, players were not so slow. Every member of the top side, Heart of Midlothian, had joined by the end of November; seven never returned, and three were killed on the first day of the Somme offensive. The Football Battalion was at the Somme as well in early 1916 and suffered many casualties. Buckley, by then a major, was injured and sent home with lung damage from poison gas and never played again.

There were 5,000 professional footballers when war broke out, and although records are not necessarily complete, it is thought that 2,000 joined the Army and crossed the English Channel. Many years later, in the 1930s, Buckley, who had researched the subject, said that 500 of the original 600 in the Football Battalion were killed in action or subsequently died from their wounds.

Elsewhere in the world, the Confederation of South American countries was founded in 1916. The influence of European migration was very helpful in the spread of the popularity of the game and, of course, Brazil and Argentina are two of the real giants of the game.

It was perhaps the railroad that had helped to develop the game in South America? Countries wanted a railroad, and British firms were at the forefront of the companies given the job of building them. That process began in the 1860s, and the workers brought their leather footballs.

With railways in place, international games began to happen fairly regularly, and the Confederation was a further step in the development of the game.

The transport network, again the railways, helped the game develop in Spain with once again British workers instrumental in the origins of the game. Atletico Bilbao adopted the colors of Durham miners whose first love was the Sunderland Club. It won the first national cup, now known as the Copa del Rey, in 1902, defeating Barcelona, and was to become the dominant force in the early days of La Liga, which was founded in 1929. The Spanish had no involvement in the first World War, and although not particularly organized a soccer country, developed enough to win the silver medal at the Olympics held in Brussels just after the War.

Peace Is Restored

The first World War had resulted in terrible loss of life with some national boundaries being redrawn, and things like sport on the one hand seemed insignificant, but on the other a release from the misery that had been created right across Europe.

Most national associations had suspended activities during the war, but competitions resumed although administratively, progress was slow because European countries still felt very raw after hostilities ceased.

The president of the French Football Federation, Jules Rimet, became FIFA's third President in 1921, while the British Associations, Brazil, and Uruguay were notable absentees when it came to membership. Soccer in the Paris Olympics of 1924 was a great success with twenty-four nations competing. A crowd of 60,000 saw Uruguay beat Switzerland 3 – 0 in the Final, and Uruguay repeated that success in Amsterdam four years later, this time defeating Argentina in the Final.

The World Cup Begins

The success of soccer at the Olympics and the drive of Jules Rimet, after whom the World Cup was later named, provided the momentum for the first World Cup which has remained the pinnacle of the game ever since. Member associations had been canvassed to ask whether they wanted a competition, and at the Congress in Amsterdam in 1928, it was agreed to hold a competition. Several European countries applied to host the competition—Sweden, Spain, the Netherlands, Italy and Hungary—but Uruguay, the reigning Olympic champions, was always the favourite. 1930 was the 10th anniversary of Uruguay independence as well, so Uruguay was confirmed as the host at the Barcelona Congress in 1929.

The economies in Europe were not strong, and the implications of clubs losing their best players for two months impacted on European participation in the first World Cup. The British Associations were not members of FIFA anyway, and in the event only four European sides entered; France, Belgium, Romania, and Yugoslavia. There were two other sides from outside South America—the USA and Mexico—that were added to seven South American countries. The first game was in Montevideo on 30th July 1930, and it was the host country that ultimately became the first World Cup holders. There was anger in Uruguay at the poor entry to the extent that the champions refused to defend the trophy four years later.

The subject of professionalism reared its head again before the Los Angeles Olympics in 1932, so football was excluded, meaning that the next meaning competition was the 1934 World Cup held in Italy. It was a knockout competition, so eight countries played just a single game before going home, Brazil and Argentina among them. Once again, the hosts were the winners, beating Czechoslovakia after extra time.

Italy retained the title in France in 1938, but the competition was fraught with problems. Argentina withdrew, Austria failed to show for the game with Sweden and Cuba, and the Dutch East Indies competed. More serious things were on the horizon.

Soccer had been played fairly informally in Africa for some time. South Africa was the first country to embrace the game, largely because of European influence, but there was no one on the Continent in a position to play in a World Cup. In Asia, the game was largely played by ex-pats, so the expansion of the game into a real worldwide affair was far away as World War II loomed.

The History of Club Soccer

As already mentioned, the economies in Europe were not strong. La Liga had started in Spain in 1929 with Barcelona winning the first championship before Atletico Bilbao and Real Madrid started to dominate. The Spanish Civil War, 1937/8 was disruptive at the problems in Europe loomed large.

Spain is regarded in today's world as one of the five major leagues of Europe, so what was happening in the other four?

The English Premier League in a way reflects regional economic strength, and of course that centers around London. Two of London's top sides, Tottenham and Chelsea, had never won the first division title before World War II, while the Manchester Clubs had made little impact. The following is a list of the clubs which had won the most titles before 1940: Aston Villa and Sunderland (both 6), Arsenal and Everton (both 5), Liverpool, Newcastle United, and Sheffield Wednesday (all 4). The industrial towns and cities of the North of England were the strength of the League. There were sides like Huddersfield Town winning three successive titles in the 1920s, and places like Burnley, Blackburn, Preston, and Sheffield prominent most years. Arsenal was an exception, but all their titles came in the 1930s, so the Club deserves a chapter to itself.

The Italian Professional League began in the 1929/30 season. Prior to that, there had been regional competitions with the ultimate national winner emerging later. Genoa was comfortably the most successful club in the years before the professional structure started, though Juventus, AC Milan, and FC Internazionale each had their names on the trophy. In the years of soccer before the league was suspended, Juventus has a run of five successive titles, with Bologna four, and Inter three successes. The game in Italy actually continued until the war got on to the doorstep, with AS Roma and Torino winning the last two titles, 1941/2, and 1942/3 respectively.

In Germany, soccer had been a regional amateur sport for some 30 years before the start of the second World War. There was a playoff system to find a national champion, and immediately prior to war breaking out, Schalke 04 could rightly claim to be the strongest club in Germany.

The French equivalent, Ligue 1, played for almost a decade until the war. There had been plenty of soccer played before that in different competitions, but the first champions in the structure known today were Lillois in 1932/3. Olympique Marseille is the only other name modern-day supporters will recognize from the winners in the other six seasons, with Sete and Sochaux-Montbeliard each being successful twice and Racing Club de Paris once.

The Arsenal Side of the 1930s

Arsenal has won the FA Cup more times than any other club. It had reached the semi-finals three times and the Final once in the late 1920s before finally winning it for the first time in 1930. It was the start of a golden decade in which the Club won the Cup a second time and the First Division title five times.

In 1930/1, Herbert Chapman's side won seven and drew one of the first eight games while Manchester United lost the first twelve games of the season. Arsenal was a free-scoring side, and by April, the first Championship was secured. Runners-up the season later, Arsenal then had a run of three successful titles, initially under Chapman, though he died in January 1934. That run was stopped by Sunderland's success, but Arsenal won the Cup as compensation, as well as getting a fifth title in the decade in the 1937/8 season.

There were several famous names in that Arsenal side, including forwards Alex James, Ted Drake, Cliff Bastin and David Jack. Chapman signed James as a 27-year-old for £8,750 from Preston North End in 1929. He was a Scottish international who played in four of those championship winning seasons, captained the Club for four and a half years, and won two FA Cups. Ted Drake initially turned Herbert Chapman down, but when the new manager, George Allison, came back to Southampton in 1934, Drake agreed to sign at a price of £6,500. He was 22 years old at the time and went on to score 42 goals in 41 games in his first season, 1934/5.

He scored 136 goals in 182 games for Arsenal before war broke out, including all seven in the 7 – 1 win over Aston Villa. Cliff Bastin was born in the same year as Drake, a left winger that Arsenal bought from Exeter City as a 17-year-old. He scored 178 goals in 395 games before injury and then the war brought an end to a glittering career. David Jack was already 29 when Chapman signed him in October 1928 from Bolton for a then record of £10,890. He was already famous for scoring the first goal in a Wembley Cup Final in Bolton's 2 – 0 win over West Ham in 1923. He played in the first three of Arsenal's championship-winning sides with his best goal return being 34 in 1930/1. He retired after the third of those successes.

World War II

World War I was restricted to Europe, but the second World War was a truly global affair, fought on land, sea, and air as far afield as the Pacific, the South Atlantic, and North Africa. Europe had been under a cloud for a while, and efforts to avoid war were in vain.

Soccer had been included in the Berlin Olympics in 1936 with amateur principles imposed. The atmosphere at those Games has often been described as sinister. Italy incidentally won the Gold Medal, but as the world lurched towards war, there was minimal international discussion on soccer, and domestic leagues knew that if peace could not be negotiated, their activities would close. As it turned out, war was declared in

September 1939, and meaningful soccer effectively finished until peace was declared.

FACTS & FIGURES

1. During World War I, on Christmas Day 1914 hostilities ceased, and a game of soccer was played between British and German soldiers.

2. Drogheda United from Ireland based its logo on the Ottoman Empire as thanks for the food it provided during the 19th Century famine.

3. Newgate Prison in London gets recognition as one of the founders of soccer in the 19th Century. Prisoners who had had their hands cut off for theft had no choice but to play ball games with their feet.

4. Professionals in the first soccer league in the USA starting in 1919 were paid 35 cents for scoring a goal.

5. The first World Cup was made from papier-mache. It was only replaced in 1950, twenty years after the first competition, because it was damaged by heavy rain.

6. Queen Elizabeth II enjoyed sport as a youngster and often disguised herself to go and watch soccer starting in the late 30s.

7. The first live televised soccer match was played at Highbury between Arsenal 1st and 2nd teams on September 16th, 1937.

8. Author, Sir Arthur Conan Doyle, who created Sherlock Holmes, founded Portsmouth FC in 1898 and became its first goalkeeper.

9. Teams in the USA first competed for a soccer cup in 1914—the Lamar Hunt US Open Cup.

10. Crossbars were only introduced in 1882. Before then, every ball going between the posts at any height counted as a goal.

11. Arthur Wharton, who was born in Ghana, was the first African professional soccer player, keeping goal for Rotherham United in 1889.

12. The first World Cup hat-trick was scored by Bert Patenaude for the USA against Paraguay in 1930.

13. Only 300 spectators watched Uruguay's victory in the Final.

14. The referee, Jean Langenus from Belgium, wore a suit jacket, tie, and golf trousers while officiating.

15. The Arsenal changed its name to just Arsenal under Herbert Chapman so as to be top of the alphabetical list of Division One Clubs.

16. Everton used to play at Anfield, now home of Liverpool FC. The club played there until moving across Stanley Park in 1892. Liverpool was founded in 1888 and took over the ground when Everton left.

17. The first balls used in China were made of sewn material filled with pebbles.

18. West Auckland FC from the North East of England was the first English side to win a European competition; it won the Sir Thomas Lipton Trophy in 1909 and 1911.

19. There was a huge score in an international between two of Europe's giants back in 1912. England beat the Netherlands 12 – 2.

20. It was not until 1913 that goalkeepers wore different colored shirts from the rest of the team.

TRIVIA QUESTIONS

1. Which of the 12 clubs that formed the first-ever Football League no longer exists?

   A   Burnley

   B   West Bromwich Albion

   C   Accrington

   D   Blackburn

   E   Stoke

2. Which country won 2 of the 3 World Cups held before the second World War?

   A   Uruguay

   B   Italy

   C   Argentina

   D   Brazil

   E   France

3. In 1929, which English Club had won the championship the most times?

   A   Aston Villa

   B   Arsenal

   C   Newcastle United

   D   Sunderland

E   Everton

4. Which Club won the first Spanish League title?

A   Real Madrid

B   Atletico Bilbao

C   Real Betis

D   Racing Santander

E   Barcelona

5. Which of these countries was not a founder member of FIFA?

A   Sweden

B   The Netherlands

C   France

D   England

E   Denmark

ANSWERS

1. C
2. B
3. A
4. E
5. D

CHAPTER 2
A Changing World

Soccer Starts Again

After peace came to the world, soccer was something that took people's minds off the years of misery. There was much rebuilding to be done in Europe, of course, and life was not easy. Soccer was a fairly cheap form of entertainment in the days before everyone had a television, and the crowds reflected that. Most of the spectators stood on terraces with a series of small barriers interspersed on the steps. Life was fairly orderly, so there were no real problems as games. There was certainly plenty of enthusiasm, but there was no suggestion that soccer was at all tribal, and segregation was not necessary. There had been enough trouble in recent years without continuing it at a game which was there to enjoy.

A New World

After the First World War, the map of Europe changed. The change that came after World War II was the Iron Curtain in Europe, behind which many East European countries came under the influence of the USSR. While that did not itself change the playing of soccer, it did have an influence on the mood of countries.

Elsewhere, the process of many colonies gaining independence from their European colonial masters began. The major impact was felt in Africa, where the British, French, Belgians, and Portuguese had held sway. To date, the continent of Africa knew the game of soccer, but outside South Africa, it had little structure. That was to change.

Asia was lagging behind in soccer terms, and it was some time before the number of countries regarding soccer as a significant game grew in any great way.

FIFA Starts to Grow

FIFA had grown to a membership of fifty-one before the outbreak of the second World War, but by 1950, that number had increased to seventy-three. FIFA played a positive role in promoting the game and encouraging associations to be formed on every continent.

It was ready to run another World Cup in 1950, which it did successfully in Brazil, and progressive thinkers within the game were looking for new ideas in how it could be promoted and expanded.

Great Britain v The Rest of Europe

137,000 spectators packed into Hampden Park in Glasgow on 10th May 1947 to watch this friendly game to celebrate the return of the Home Nations to FIFA. Walter Winterbottom managed the GB side and selected five Englishmen, three Scots, two Welsh, and one Northern Ireland players.

GB Team: Frank Swift (Manchester City and England), George Hardwick (capt.) (Middlesbrough & England), Jack Vernon (West Bromwich Albion & Northern Ireland), Ron Burgess (Tottenham Hotspur & Wales), Tommy Lawton (Chelsea & England), Billy Liddell (Liverpool & Scotland), Stanley Matthews (Blackpool & England), Wilf Mannion (Middlesbrough & England), Archie Macaulay (Arsenal & Scotland), Billy Hughes (Birmingham City & Wales). Billy Steel (Morton & Scotland).

The Rest of Europe team was selected by the Swiss manger, Karl Rappan, and players came from nine countries across Europe, including Johnny Carey of Manchester United and Ireland. The team in full: Willi Steffen (Switzerland), Johnny Carey, Julien Da Rui (France), Gunnar Gren (Sweden), Victor Lambrechts (Belgium), Josef Ludl (Czechoslovakia), Gunnar Nordahl (Sweden), Carlo Parola (Italy), Poul Pedersen (Denmark), Carl Praest (Denmark), Faas Wilkes (The Netherlands).

The game itself was fairly one-sided, finishing 6 – 1 to Great Britain. Wilf Mannion gave the home side an early lead, and then he restored that lead with a penalty after Gunnar Nordahl had briefly equalized. Tommy Lawton with two, Billy Steel, and an own goal by Carlo Parola completed the scoring.

Two footnotes to the game.

Wilf Mannion many years later described how he was told to bring white shorts and navy-blue socks and then was given his navy-blue shirt on arrival. He traveled third class on the train from Middlesbrough on England's north-east coast across to Glasgow, standing most of the way. That doesn't sound much like how professional soccer players travel in the modern day.

Sadly, Frank Swift was killed in the Munich Air Disaster in 1958.

Stanley Matthews' Cup Final

One of the best players that England ever produced was Stanley Matthews. He played 54 times for England at a time when internationals were less frequent. He was born in 1915, so he was already 30 years old when soccer resumed after the war. He was knighted while he was still playing professional football at the age of 50, in 1965, and was the first European Footballer of the Year. In all his time on the field, he was never booked. He won two Second Division titles with Stoke City, the second one towards the very end of his career.

He had begun his career with Stoke City as a 17-year-old and finished there in 1965, but during a time in the intervening years, he played for Blackpool for whom he strove to win an FA Cup winners' medal. Blackpool had lost in the 1948 Final and the 1951 Final, so most people thought the chances of Stanley picking up that elusive winners' medal had gone. Blackpool reached the Final again though in 1953, but trailing 3 – 1 against

Bolton Wanderers, it looked like Matthews was going to get his third losers' medal. Matthews took over and three goals came in the later stages, two for Stan Mortensen and one for Bill Perry from another Matthews' cross.

Matthews returned to Stoke in 1961.

No one will ever match his longevity in terms of playing professional soccer at the highest level. He was a fitness fanatic and well ahead of his time in terms of diet and training.

Hungary

Hungary was the reigning Olympic Champion in 1953 when it came to play England at Wembley on 25th November. England had never lost a home international to a non-British team, but that was a record that fell quite spectacularly in what has been billed as the "Match of the Century."

England had a high opinion of itself despite losing to the USA three seasons earlier in the World Cup, but there was usually an excuse whenever it had a setback. It was hard to find one in the game against Hungary. There were many famous names in the England team; four of Blackpool's FA Cup winning side, Billy Wright, Jimmy Dickinson of Portsmouth, and England's 1966 World Cup winning manager Alf Ramsey. Seven of Hungary's eleven played for Budapest Honved SE, including the legendary Ferenc Puskas.

Hungary had the game won comfortably by the hour, having

already scored six, and seemed to ease off in the later stages but still won 6 – 3. Tactics found England out from the start. With Hungary playing a false Number 9, Nandor Hidegkuti, the English centre-half Harry Johnston had no one to mark and didn't know what to do. Hidegkuti actually scored in the first minute. Although England was level through Sewell after 15 minutes, the Hungarians were soon 4 – 1 up with goals from Puskas (2) and a further one from Hidegkuti. Stan Mortensen pulled one back by half-time but it was the Hungarians again on the resumption, goals from Boszik and Hidegkuti completing his hat-trick. Ramsey's reply with a penalty was scant consolation.

The Hungarian players appeared to wear random numbers; it was all very confusing.

The following year, Hungary emphasized its superiority by beating England 7 – 1 and not surprisingly was installed as the firm favorite for that year's World Cup in Switzerland.

Germany Opens its Account

Recovery from the War was continuing, and by 1954, the World Cup was played in a better atmosphere than the one four years earlier. It was held in Switzerland, and it was the first time in the history of the Cup that the hosts were unable to make progress to the later stages.

While Uruguay was the holder, undoubtedly, Hungary was the favorite going into the Competition. There were 16 teams in the

Cup with some nations having to go through a qualification process to reach Switzerland. They played in four Groups of four teams with the top two in each league going forward to the knockout stages. Holders Uruguay safely qualified for the quarter finals and then beat England to qualify for the semi-finals.

Undoubtedly, one of the best games in the tournament was Hungary's 4 – 2 win over Brazil in Berne on 27th June. Austria had beaten hosts Switzerland 7 – 5 the day before in Lausanne. The last semi-finalist was Germany who defeated Yugoslavia 2 – 0.

A few days later, Germany easily disposed of Austria 6 – 1, but Hungary needed extra time to beat Uruguay 4 – 2. The South Americans lost the third/fourth playoff match before the Final was held on the 4th of July. The crowd of 62,500 did not match that of the previous Final in the huge Maracanã Stadium in Rio de Janeiro, but it was capacity with not a space in sight.

Within eight minutes, Hungary was two up through Puskas and Czibor, so the favorites' tag looked to be justified, but Germany replied through Max Morlock just two minutes later and then was level when Helmut Rahn equalized after eighteen minutes. The game was hard fought with the winner for Germany coming with just six minutes to go with a second from Rahn.

It was the start of a wonderful international record for Germany. It won the Cup a second time as West Germany in 1974 and has subsequently won it on two more occasions as well as being losing finalists three times.

A Teenager in Sweden

Few who watched the World Cup in Sweden in 1958 would realize that a young teenager in the Brazilian side would become on the most famous names in sport. Edson Arantes do Nascimento had been born on October 23, 1940, in Três Corações, Brazil. He became known to the world as Pele and is widely regarded as one of the finest soccer players ever to play the game.

Unlike many South Americans in the modern day who head for Europe, he played professionally for Santos in Brazil for most of his career until a spell late at New York Cosmos in the USA. His father was a soccer player, but it was difficult to make a living, so Pele knew real poverty, learning the game with a ball that was merely rags stuffed into a sock in the streets of Bauru where the family moved when he was young.

As a teenager, he showed real promise, and Waldemar de Brito, a former international and now a coach, recommended him to Santos in Sao Paulo when he was just 15. His first senior goal was just after his 16th birthday, and he finished the season top scorer and was selected by Brazil.

Sweden was the next country to see his magic as he scored a hat-trick against France in the World Cup semi-final, a 5 – 2 wins for Brazil who, remember, at that time had yet to win the World Cup. He added two more against the hosts in the Final at the tender age of 17, a young phenomenon.

Santos was able to hold on to its star partly because of lucrative matches against teams around the world. Brazil retained the Cup in 1962 in Chile, though Pele was injured after just two games. In England in 1966, there was some questionable refereeing as Brazil did not get out of the Group stage. Pele had his revenge in 1970 with a third win, scoring in the 4 – 1 win over Italy in the Final in Mexico City, 12 years after his brace in the 1958 Final.

He briefly retired in 1974 before agreeing to play for New York Cosmos with his final game being in October 1977 against his old club, Santos. His record is astonishing; 1,281 goals in 1,363 games.

The Munich Air Disaster

The terrible air disaster that killed so many of the Manchester United team and officials was a dark day in soccer history. Manchester United had won the English First Division in 1956/7, and its players and officials had just beaten Red Star Belgrade in the quarter final of the European Cup. The plane stopped in Munich for refueling on 6th February 1958 but crashed on takeoff with twenty of the party of forty-four killed immediately and three more dying in hospital from their injuries. In total, eight of the side died, among them young star Duncan Edwards and center-forward Tommy Taylor, and others were too badly injured to play again. Exceptions were the future English star Bobby Charlton, goalkeeper Harry Gregg, and defender Bill Foulkes.

Manchester United was managed by Matt Busby, who had taken the job in 1945 when soccer resumed after the Second World War. He led his team to the FA Cup in 1948, and four years later, Manchester United won its first League Championship in 41 years. In the mid-1950s, his team was called the "Busby Babes" because the average age was just 22. It failed in its attempt to do the "English double" by losing in the FA Cup Final against Aston Villa but was the first English Club to enter the European Cup the following season despite opposition from the Football League.

Busby survived though badly injured and finally agreed to remain as manager. Incidentally, a completely new United side was quickly assembled and was losing finalists in that terrible season's FA Cup, beaten by Bolton Wanderers.

The Club fully recovered, and its subsequent success makes it one of the most successful clubs in world soccer history.

Real Madrid

Real Madrid was one of the founder members of the Spanish League and played with some success prior to the war, but it took the Club a few years after the League resumed to win the Title again. Once it did, it was eligible to play in the first-ever European Club Champions Cup in 1955/6. The impact it made was quite astonishing with the Spanish Club winning it in each of the first five years.

While many highlights the 1960 win, 7 – 3 over Eintracht

Frankfurt in front of over 127,000 spectators at Hampden Park in Glasgow, as one of the best games ever played, it was also the fifth of those wins and the previous four deserve mention.

1956	Real Madrid 4	Reims 3	Paris
1957	Real Madrid 2	Fiorentina 0	Madrid
1958	Real Madrid 3	Milan 2 a.e.t.	Brussels
1959	Real Madrid 2	Stade Reims 0	Stuttgart

The Argentinian Alfredo Di Stéfano and Ferenc Puskas, signed from Honved, were the standout performers in a side full of great players. Di Stefano scored three of the goals in that Final, Puskas the other four, but both were approaching their mid-thirties, so it was not surprising that the run came to an end. Di Stefano had been seen when Real hosted a tournament during its 50th Anniversary and signed up as quickly as possible. He went on the win two Ballon d'Ors, 1957 and 1959, with Real's Frenchman Raymond Kopa winning in the intervening year. After that fifth success, Real then won the first-ever Intercontinental Cup against Penarol de Montevideo 5 – 1.

Real had only one further win in the next thirty-seven years before three wins at the turn of the Century and more success recently.

Tottenham's ''Double''

No Club had won the English League and Cup, the ''Double'', in the 20th Century, and it had only been achieved once before in history, Aston Villa in 1897. That was to change in the 1960/1 season when Tottenham Hotspur went to Wembley for the Cup Final having already clinched the League. The opponents that day were Leicester City, whose captain Frank McLintock was to enjoy similar success with Arsenal a decade later. Much had happened in the season before that day in May.

Spurs' Manager was Bill Nicholson who had taken over in October 1958, and in his second season, Spurs briefly flirted with relegation. The signing of Dave Mackay from Hearts in Scotland stiffened the defense, and Nicholson added inside forward John White from Falkirk a year later; Spurs finished 3rd in 1959/60.

Tottenham, led by its Irish captain, Danny Blanchflower, won the first Eleven games of the league season in 1960/1 before drawing with Manchester City. It was the 17th game when the team had its first defeat, 2 – 1 against Sheffield Wednesday. Just before Christmas, Spurs led 4 – 0 against Burnley but only managed a draw. Leading by 11 points at the turn of the year, the Championship looked a formality.

The FA Cup campaign began early in January, a 3 – 2 win against Charlton Athletic followed by an easy win 5 – 1 when hosting Crewe Alexandra. After winning away at Aston Villa, Spurs faced Second Division Sunderland at Roker Park in the quarter finals. After getting a 1 – 1 draw, somewhat fortunate reports say, there was no problem back at White Hart Lane 5 – 0.

Semi-finals are at neutral grounds, with Spurs beating Burnley 3 − 0 at Villa Park in front of a crowd of 70,000.

Spurs' League form was patchy in the second half of the season; half an eye on the "Double"? The lead was just 3 points by Easter. The lead was increased once more, allowing Spurs to lose two of its last three games and still win the Championship, but the points' record was gone. Now for the FA Cup Final!

Leicester City had had a difficult run to Wembley, including an abandonment for a waterlogged pitch and replays against Birmingham and Barnsley in the 5th and 6th Rounds, respectively. The semi-final against Sheffield United went to extra time in the second replay at St. Andrews, Birmingham, before Leicester won 2 − 0.

The Final was goalless at halftime, but Bobby Smith gave Spurs the lead after 66 minutes. Terry Dyson added a second soon afterwards, and the historic "Double" was completed.

UEFA

FIFA had been born at the beginning of the 20th Century, but as the game grew, there was a feeling that there was a need for a body which joined the countries in Europe and looks after their interests. The impetus for such a body came from France, and more specifically Henri Delaunay. He was the French National Association General Secretary who as early as 1927 had written to FIFA suggesting a European Cup. He was supported by the

Austrian Hugo Meisi. That came to nothing and, of course, there was a great deal of history in the intervening years.

Early in the 1950s, Delaunay, the former Italian Football Federation secretary and president, Dr Ottorino Barassi, and the Belgian, José Crahay, were prime movers in seeking a European body. In 1953, FIFA approved the formation of Continental Soccer Associations, so in 1954, the Union des Associations Européennes de Football UEFA was born and held its first assembly in Basel.

At the time, there were thirty-one members of UEFA.

Delaunay died a year later, but his son Pierre was to become a driving force towards a European Nations Competition. However, the European Champion Clubs' Cup began before the Nations Competition finally took place.

The UEFA Cup Winners' Cup (European Cup Winners' Cup), where domestic cup winners would play in a knockout competition, was first played in 1960/61, and the first European/South American Cup, between the winners of the champion clubs' competitions in Europe and South America, also started in 1960.

Only half of UEFA's membership sought to play in the first European Nations' Cup. It did not include three of Europe's "giants"—Italy, that had already won the World Cup twice, and England and West Germany, who were to do so in the next fifteen years. That was seventeen teams which was one more than was required. A qualifying playoff was therefore needed, and Czechoslovakia beat the Republic of Ireland in the content.

Russia was the venue for the first game in the competition with the opening game on 28th September 1958, seeing Anatoli Ilyin scoring for Russia after just four minutes as Russia went on to beat Hungary 3 – 1. The winner was not decided for a further twenty-two months.

Russia was ultimately to win the competition, beating Yugoslavia in France 2 – 1 after extra time. Czechoslovakia and France were the defeated semi-finalists.

Africa

Soccer was brought to Africa by Europeans, and with the only requirement being an open space, it soon became popular on a fairly unstructured basis. The formation of soccer clubs within cities was regularly sponsored by major companies as well as on government initiative. Police, army, and railroad teams formed in many countries, with national teams selected from here.

Leagues were still not in place, but they were to gradually appear with momentum being added as independence was granted.

The Confédération Africaine de Football (CAF) was formed in 1957 with the approval of FIFA. Its aim was to improve the quality of the sport and its representation on a wider level. It has certainly succeeded. Initially, there were just four members, but moving forward to today, there are fifty-five, such has been the growth from such small beginnings.

North America

The North American Football Confederation (NAFC) was founded in 1946 with three members: Mexico—the strongest in soccer terms of the three, the USA, and Canada. It was one of three associations covering soccer in North and Central America, as well as the Caribbean.

The Central American Football Union with seven members and the Caribbean countries formed the Confederación Centroamericana y del Caribe de Fútbol (CCCF) which merged with the NAFC at a meeting in Mexico City in 1961 to form the Confederation of North, Central American, and Caribbean Association Football, commonly described merely as CONCACAF.

A Rivalry Is Born

Japan and the Korean Republic played an international in the Spring of 1954. The World Cup's influence was spreading, and there was a place available in the 16-team competition for a qualifier from Asia. Israel was part of the European system and Thailand withdrew, so it left Japan and the Korean Republic to fight it out for that precious place.

The original intention was that it would be played over two legs, home and away, but Syngman Rhee, the Korean President, refused to allow Japan—such recent invaders of Korea—to land in his country again. As a result, both games were scheduled for Japan. The first game was on 7th March, with Korea winning 5 –

1, and the second a week later would have been a mere formality if the result was decided on goals scored, but it wasn't. A Japanese victory by any score would mean a third game.

Japan opened the scoring through Toshio Iwatani before Korea struck twice through Chung Nam-Sick and Choi Jung-Min to lead at half-time. Iwatani equalized on the hour. Japan could not force a winner, as it pressed strongly in the later stages despite almost scoring with five minutes to go when Lee Jong-Kap had to clear off the line.

Korea found it difficult in Switzerland, suffering heavy defeats by Hungary and Turkey, but it had made history.

The Asian Cup

The Asian Football Confederation (AFC) was formed at a meeting in Manila in 1954 during the Asian Games. FIFA was happy to approve it and did so in June of the same year.

The Asian Cup was introduced as a competition in 1956 at the instigation of the newly formed confederation to oversee the sport in Asia.

The Korean Republic won the first two cups with Choi Jung-Min, who had featured in the side which represented Asia in the 1954 World Cup, very much its star.

FACTS & FIGURES

1. Derby County has its only FA Cup success on the resumption of the competition after the War, beating Charlton Athletic 2 – 1 after extra time.

2. Newcastle United won the FA Cup three times between 1951 and 1955 but have not won it since.

3. The European Cup for Champion Clubs was first played for in the 1955/6 season with Real Madrid running out as winners.

4. Floodlights began to be installed in England with friendlies against foreign sides attracting huge crowds. In one such game, English champions Wolverhampton Wanderers beat Honved of Budapest 2 – 1 in December 1954, six months after five of the Honved side had been in the Hungary team that beat England 7 – 1.

5. The Latin Cup preceded the European Cup and was played between the Champions of France, Italy, Spain, and Portugal. The first Latin Cup was played in Spain in 1949 with Barcelona beating Sporting Lisbon 2 – 1 in the Final. It finished two seasons after the introduction of the European Cup.

6. Chelsea won the English First Division for the first time in its history and was the first English Club eligible for the newly formed European Cup. Pressure from the Football League meant it did not enter.

7. The German National team was only reformed in 1949, four years after the end of the war, but the country was now divided into two.

8. Germany was not allowed to enter the 1950 World Cup, which was won by Uruguay in front of a record 200,000 crowd in Rio de Janeiro in the Maracanã Stadium.

9. The Nigerian Football Federation was formed in 1945, with the national team starting four years later.

10. Fifty-two South Africans played professional football in England between 1945 and 1960. Eleven of them played for Charlton Athletic including Stuart Leary who also played professional cricket.

11. England beat Scotland 8 – 0 in an unofficial international at the end of the war at Maine Road, Manchester, yet manager Walter Winterbottom was strongly criticized for directing play towards Denis Compton, the Arsenal left winger who also played cricket for England. The crowds had come to see Stanley Matthews critics said, but he was double-marked leaving space elsewhere.

12. Bert Trautmann was a prisoner of war but stayed on in

England after the war finished and became a fine goalkeeper for Manchester City. He won a winners' medal against Birmingham City in the 1956 FA Cup Final, only to discover he had broken his neck during the game but had played on. He finally retired from football in 1964.

13. Billy Wright, captain of Wolverhampton Wanderers, English champions in 1957/8 and 1958/9, was captain of England and the first man to win 100 international caps.

14. David Whelan broke his leg in the first half of Blackburn Rovers FA Cup Final against Wolverhampton Wanderers in 1960. There were no substitutes in those days, and his team lost 3 – 0. He later became a successful businessman and bought non-League, Wigan Athletic. Wigan rose through the Leagues to the Premier League and caused one of the modern-day shocks by beating Manchester City in the 2013 Cup Final.

15. Alfredo di Stefano was an early example of someone who played internationally for two countries. He was born in Buenos Aires in 1926 and made his debut for Argentina in 1947. After signing for Real Madrid, he took Spanish citizenship and went on to play for his adopted country 31 times, scoring 23 goals.

16. Welshman, John Charles, who had a successful career in England and Italy, was equally at home at center-forward and center-half. He was the first foreign player inducted

into the Italian Hall of Fame following his time at Juventus. Born in Swansea in 1931, he was capped at 18 and helped Wales push Brazil in the quarter-finals of the 1958 World Cup Finals in Sweden.

17. When Raich Carter complained that when he passed to Stanley Matthews, he never got the ball back. England Manager Walter Winterbottom's response was that he should head for the penalty area because there would be a cross coming over.

18. The Turkish League began in 1958, even though the oldest teams date back to the beginning of the Century: Besiktas (1903), Galatasary (1905), Fenerbahce (1907). Each have a huge fan base across the country even though the League covers most of the vast country of Turkey.

19. Soccer was never especially popular in New Zealand, perhaps because it is relatively remote. The first European visitors to New Zealand were FK Austria in 1957, with an England XI following on in 1961.

20. Although there were three different soccer associations in South Africa, representing the Bantus, the Coloureds, and the Whites, FIFA only recognized the "white body", FASA, in 1958. The first professional club league started the following year with only white South Africans eligible to play.

TRIVIA QUESTIONS

1. Which survivor of the Munich Air Crash went on to play more than 100 times for England and was in the 1966 World Cup winning team?

   A   Bill Foulkes

   B   Duncan Edwards

   C   Harry Gregg

   D   Bobby Charlton

   E   Tommy Taylor

2. How old was Stanley Matthews when he made his last appearance in the English First Division?

   A   40

   B   45

   C   47

   D   48

   E   50

3. Which Hungarian player scored a hat-trick at Wembley in 1953?

   A   Ferenc Puskas

   B   Nandor Hidegkuti

   C   Joszef Boszik

   D   Sandor Kocsis

E Zoltan Czibor

4. Which player stood on his way to an important soccer match?

    A Wilf Mannion
    B Tommy Lawton
    C Billy Liddell
    D Billy Steel
    E Stanley Matthews

5. Pele played for which South American country?

    A Uruguay
    B Argentina
    C Brazil
    D Chile
    E Paraguay

ANSWERS

1. D
2. E
3. B
4. A
5. C

CHAPTER 3

TWO DECADES OF CLASSIC SOCCER

The Swinging Sixties is an often-used phrase. Life became more informal, and most would certainly say more fun. There was yet to be the huge increase in readily available air travel for the masses, but society was becoming more mobile. That was reflected in general behavior and use of leisure time. Soccer benefitted as it became easier to see soccer on television, and what a treat some of the great sides provided.

European Cup Winners Cup

The original European Champions Cup was a much smaller competition than it is today. Only the actual domestic champions qualified, and it was a knockout competition. One introduction that meant there was more cross-border activity with the European Cup Winners Cup that was first played in the season following Real Madrid winning its fifth successive European title.

Many countries had had cup competitions before they introduced leagues, so it was a natural progression, even if the winners were not awarded similar plaudits to those taking the main trophy.

Fiorentina was the first winner, and Real's city rivals, Atletico, was the next. There was a good deal of British success in the first decade with Tottenham, West Ham, and Chelsea all winning at the first opportunity.

West Ham's success was interesting. It is a club without any domestic league honors but many famous footballers, including three of the England side that won the 1966 World Cup, skipper Bobby Moore, hat-trick hero Geoff Hurst, and England's other scorer, Martin Peters. West Ham had beaten Manchester United in the semi-final and went on to defeat Preston North End 3 − 2 at Wembley. The Cup Winners Cup Final was also scheduled for Wembley, where West Ham beat TSV 1860 Munich 2 − 0.

Benfica

Portuguese champions Benfica was the team that prevented a sixth successive Real Madrid Cup. It beat its close Spanish rival instead, Barcelona, 3 − 2, and Real itself 5 − 3 a year later.

In 1961, Real Madrid qualified as holders and Barcelona as Spanish champions. Barcelona was to eliminate Real Madrid on the way to the Final. Benfica beat Rapid Wien in the Semis. Kocsis put Barcelona ahead in the Final, but goals from Aguas, his eighth in the Cup that season, an own goal from goalkeeper, Ramalletts and Coluna put the Portuguese in control. Czibor, the old Hungarian star replied, but Benfica took the Cup.

In 1962, a young star firmly established himself on the stage—Eusebio, whose two goals helped Benfica retain the Cup despite a hat-trick from Puskas. Real had actually taken an early two-goal lead and still led at the break 3 − 1. Benfica scored four without reply in the second half including the final two by Eusebio.

While Africa had yet to produce any soccer stars to this point, Eusebio, born in 1942, in Lourenço Marques, Mozambique, one of the Portuguese colonies, was certainly a fine player. He had a great career for Benfica and Portugal but could not add to his winners' medals.

The Milan Giants

One of the great rivalries in club soccer is Internazionale Milan and AC Milan, yet they share the same stadium, the San Siro. Colours have to change as the respective teams play at home, and once a season, each takes the away dressing room as their meeting is designated as a home or away fixture against close rivals.

Both of these Italian "greats" started to make an impact in European history in the early 60s, with AC Milan now having seven European Cup wins in all.

AC Milan took the Cup for the first time to prevent Benfica's third successive win. Anderlecht had eliminated Real Madrid in the early stages. Feyenoord and Dundee were two unlikely semi-finalists, but they lost to Benfica and AC Milan, respectively.

There were several names in the Italian side that the world would hear more about: Cesare Maldini was now a veteran, but there were Trappatoni, in his prime, Altafini, who scored both Milan's goals to make it a record 14 in that year's competition, and teenage sensation Gianni Rivera. Despite Eusebio giving Benfica the lead at Wembley, the Italians prevailed.

The following year, it was its neighbors Inter that won the Cup. Real Madrid knocked the holders out before the quarter final stage, and it beat Zurich 6 – 0 to reach the Final. Having beaten Dortmund 2 – 0 in the other semi-final, Inter beat Real Madrid 3 – 1 in the Final to win the Cup for the first time; Mazzola scored two of the three before Felo gave Real consolation.

Inter beat Liverpool 4 – 3 on aggregate in the semi-final before retaining the Cup the following year by beating Benfica by a single goal scored by Jair just before the break.

The brief Italian domination ended the next year when Real Madrid beat Inter in the semi-final and went on to win its 6th Cup.

North Korea

Africa as a continent had not really impacted on the World Cup. Egypt's appearance in 1934 had very much been a "one off", and the next African team to appear in the World's premier competition was Morocco in 1970. Asia had been limited as well, but when North Korea set foot in England for the World

Cup of 1966, there was a shock in store.

Korea was drawn in the North-East Group with Chile, Russia, and Italy playing at Middlesbrough's Ayresome Park and Sunderland's Roker Park that was also scheduled for a quarter final for the Group winner. North Korea could not manage that, but its 1 – 0 win at Ayresome Park over Italy, including a host of famous names, was an astonishing result. It meant it qualified for the quarter final against Portugal at Goodison Park in Liverpool, and a shock looked on the cards again as it led 3 – 0 only for the Portuguese star Eusebio to take control to win 5 – 3. The fairytale was over, but it has never been forgotten.

The Cup Comes Home?

England had seen itself as the home of soccer, had justifiably been accused of being fairly aloof over the years, and certainly wasn't pro-active in suggesting change. It did not send a team to early World Cups, and prevented its clubs playing in the early European Club Cups as well. However, an Englishman, Stanley Rous, became FIFA President in 1961, and England was awarded the 1966 World Cup.

The host's progress was not without incident. The tournament kicked off with a 0 – 0 draw at Wembley, but England safely qualified for the quarter finals at Wembley against Argentina. The South American's captain, Antonio Rattin, was sent off in a feisty game that England won with a single goal by Geoff Hurst as the game approached the last ten minutes. The semi-final win over Portugal was equally close, 2 – 1 with West Germany awaiting in the Final.

Whether Geoff Hurst's shot crossed the line to put England 3 – 2 ahead in extra time is still the subject of debate. Germany had taken an early lead, and after England scored through Hurst and Peters, equalized in injury time. Hurst's own third with the last kick of the game was almost a sideline.

Celtic

No British side had won the European Club Cup when the English national team won the World Cup. The honor of being European Club Champion came from elsewhere; Scotland, with Celtic taking the Cup with a tight 2 – 1 win over two -time champions Internazionale Milan, who had beaten holders Real Madrid in the quarter final.

Celtic has recently emerged under manager Jock Stein to win the first of a number of Scottish titles, but it was the underdog for this game. It appeared to have an easier route to the Final, beating Dukla Prague in the semi-finals to qualify for the Final to be played in the National Stadium in Lisbon. Inter was certainly the favorite. Italian football had a reputation for skill but also organized defense, so when Inter went ahead with a penalty in just the 7th minute through Sandro Mazolla, it seemed that Celtic had a real challenge on its hands.

Inter appeared unconcerned with Celtic attacks until the 63rd minute when full back Tommy Gemmell's shot hit the back of the net. The winner for Celtic came with just six minutes to go through Stephen Chalmers.

A Night at Wembley

Manchester United was to put an English name on the Cup a season later with Benfica suffering another Final defeat after its two early successes in the 60s. Many of the Benfica side, including Eusebio, had lost in the World Cup semi-final defeat that Portugal suffered two years previously at Wembley while Bobby Charlton and Nobby Stiles turned out for United. Wembley was once again the venue with United finally running out 4 – 1 winners, with three goals scored in extra time.

It was just after the 10th Anniversary of the Munich Air Disaster, and over the decade, the Club had assembled a talented team including a Munich survivor Bobby Charlton, Scotsman Denis Law, and George Best, the Ulsterman whose United career had begun when he was just 17.

Charlton had scored in the early in the second half with Jaime Garcia equalizing with just over ten minutes to go. In injury time, United took control with goals from Best (92), Charlton (98), and Brian Kidd (95). It was a great reward for Matt Busby, another survivor of Munich.

The Arsenal Double

When your closest rivals have done the English League and Cup "double", the sooner you can match that achievement the better. When Tottenham achieved this in the early 60s, it presented Arsenal with a real challenge. It was one it met in the 1970/1 season.

Bertie Mee was the manager who goes down in Arsenal history as being the first to achieve this, though more recently Arsene Wenger has done it twice. It was indeed sweet for Arsenal that it clinched the league title at the home of its biggest rivals, White Hart Lane with a 1 – 0 win just five days before it was scheduled to play Liverpool at Wembley in the FA Cup Final. It had taken a replay in the semi-final against Stoke City to get there.

The Final was another tough and close game, going to extra time still scoreless. Steve Heighway scored as soon as extra time started, but Eddie Kelly had Arsenal level soon afterwards. Charlie George scored the winner. Frank McLintock, Arsenal captain, had lost five times previously at Wembley. How about sixth time lucky?

Bob Stokoe and Sunderland

Bob Stokoe had been a stalwart of the Newcastle United FA Cup winning side of the 1950s. When he took over close rivals Sunderland in November 1972, he found the team in the bottom half of the Second Division. What was to happen over the remaining weeks of the season was quite remarkable.

A Cup run is often seen as a break from problems in a league, but when Sunderland drew Manchester City away in the fifth round, it seemed that Sunderland's run would finish. City were second favorites for the Cup and Sunderland 100/1. After drawing at Maine Road 2 – 2, Sunderland won the replay 3 – 1 to reach the last eight. The sixth-round draw gave them a home tie against Luton which was won 2 – 0. The other three semi-finalists all wanted Sunderland, and as it turned out, the draw pitted Sunderland against Arsenal, the "double winners" from two seasons before. The game at Hillsborough, Sheffield, was a tense affair, especially after Charlie George scored with just a few minutes to go to bring the London team back into the game at 2 – 1 after earlier Sunderland goals from Vic Halom and Billy Hughes. Sunderland held out to reach Wembley, where the opposition Leeds United awaited, arguably the most consistently strong side in recent seasons.

Don Revie, the manager and ex-Sunderland footballer, had amassed a side that was difficult to beat, and Leeds had won the FA Cup the previous season, beating Arsenal. Just before the half hour, Ian Porterfield volleyed into the Leeds goal from a Dave Watson knockdown, and a shock was on the cards. In the second half, Sunderland's goalkeeper, Jimmy Montgomery made an astonishing double save from Trevor Cherry and Peter Lorimer, and Leeds rarely threatened again. The sight of Bob

Stokoe in his trilby hat running to embrace Montgomery at the final whistle is still regularly played when programmes cover the FA Cup.

It was a major shock, and there have been others since but few match Sunderland 1973.

South America

The Copa Libertadores began as a seven-team competition and grew impressively from there. The size and terrain of South America has always made it a major challenge for any club playing away from home. It may be the heat of the equator or the altitude of the Andes that adds to the difficulty of playing away.

While Brazil and Argentina are the two strongest countries in South America, the winners of the Copa have come from many different countries.

There had been interclub games from as early as 1948, but it was on the initiative of José Ramos de Freitas of Brazil that discussions took place with Paraguay, Uruguay, Argentina, and Chile for a new competition. In all ten countries met in Caracas in Venezuela in 1959, with the hosts abstaining and Uruguay voting against a competition. Eight were in favor, and it began in April 1960.

The winner was to meet the European Champion Club, incidentally to get an unofficial World Champion.

Uruguay had voted against the competition, but that did not stop it competing. The first game was between its Montevideo Club, Peñarol , who played the Bolivian club Jorge Wilstermann. Peñarol went on to win the Final against Olimpia of Paraguay to become the first champion.

Ajax

Feyenoord was the first Dutch team to win the European Cup, but it is Ajax of Amsterdam that is best remembered for its feat of winning three successive titles. It had a number of very talented individuals, some of whom were lured away from the Netherlands by the riches of clubs elsewhere in Europe, but not before Ajax found its place in soccer history.

Ajax was runner-up in 1969, and after Feyenoord won in 1970, beating Celtic of Scotland in extra time, Ajax then won in each of the next three seasons. Johan Cruyff, who then moved on to Barcelona, was perhaps its best player, but there were several more, and the quality of soccer it played had boded well for the chances of Netherlands in the forthcoming World Cup in Germany.

The 3 results were:

1971	Ajax 2 (Van Dijk, Kapsos (og))	Panathinaikos 0	London
1972	Ajax 2 (Cruyff 2)	Internazionale 0	Rotterdam
1973	Ajax 1 (Rep)	Juventus 0	Belgrade

The following season, Ajax lost to CSKA Sofia after extra time in just the Second Round.

Dutch Frustration

Brazil came to West Germany as World Cup Champions in 1974, but once again it failed to retain the Cup. The final was played out between two near neighbors, the hosts and the Netherlands, who despite scoring from a penalty though Johan Neeskens right at the beginning ultimately lost 2 – 1. Paul Breitner equalized with a German penalty, with Gerd Muller scoring the winner still in the first half.

The competition itself saw Australia, Zaire, and Haiti for the first time, with Scotland the sole "Home Union" representatives. None was able to get past the first stage even though Scotland was undefeated in its three games. The Netherlands disposed of Brazil who had also beaten Argentina in the second group stages. Poland took third place defeating Brazil 1 – 0 in the playoff.

The Netherlands was to fall just short again four years later in 1978, when it lost to hosts Argentina 3 – 1 in Buenos Aires after extra time. An exciting playoff between Tunisia and Morocco resulted in Morocco going to Argentina and getting a first win for the African continent; it beat Mexico 3 – 1.

Scotland was again the only representative from the Home Unions in the early stages, but it was not enough to take it forward. Former winners Italy and Brazil played off for third place, Brazil winning 2 – 1.

Bayern Munich

Bayern Munich's record in the European Club Championship is impressive, and its success effectively began in 1974 when it won its first title. It beat Ajax's conqueror, CSKA Sofia, in the quarter finals, Ujpest of Hungary in the Semis, and Atletico Madrid in Brussels in a replay two days after the two had drawn $1 - 1$ after extra time. Bayern had only equalized in the 119th minute of that first game. In the second game, the result was rarely in doubt with Hoeness and Muller both scoring twice.

It retained the Cup the following year, beating the English champions Leeds United $2 - 0$ in Paris with goals from Roth and Muller again. Roth's goal a year later in Glasgow was enough to get Bayern their own treble, the French champions St. Etienne being the opponents.

Dynamo Kiev ended Bayern's hopes of a fourth win at the quarter final stage, and the era of the English began.

Liverpool

Liverpool is England's most successful club in European football, and that success began in the 1970s. It had not won the English First Division for many years, but not only did it win four domestic titles in the 70s, it won two UEFA Cups and the big prize, the European Cup itself, twice.

The first European Cup win was against Borussia Monchengladbach in 1977, 3 – 1, in Rome, and it added a second success a year later when beating Club Brugge 1 – 0 at Wembley.

Liverpool had won its first European Trophy in 1973 against the same opposition in the newly formed UEFA Cup which followed the scrapping of the invitation-only Inter City Fairs Cup. The previous season was the first for that competition, Tottenham defeating Wolverhampton Wanderers over the two-leg final. Goals from Smith, Neal, and McDermott won the European Cup for Liverpool. Ironically, it was Brugge whom Liverpool beat in 1976 for its second UEFA Cup, and in 1978, a goal from Kenny Dalglish, who had been signed from Celtic to replace Kevin Keegan, meant Liverpool retained the trophy.

There was no third win in a row because Liverpool lost in the early stages the following year to Nottingham Forest, the new English champions, but that is for the next chapter, because English teams won the Cup for six seasons in a row.

Kevin Keegan

Few Englishmen have been a great success when playing for clubs abroad, but one who most certainly was, was Kevin Keegan who after making his name at Liverpool won the Ballon D'Or twice while playing in the Bundesliga for Hamburg which was enjoying its most successful era in its history. He moved to Liverpool after starting his career at Scunthorpe United and scored in the 1974 FA Cup final in the 3 – 0 win over Newcastle

United, whom he was later to play for and then manage.

He played in Liverpool's first European Cup success before leaving for Hamburg where Bayern Munich had been the dominant force through the decade. To win successive Ballon D'Ors with a relatively unfashionable club was quite a feat. Hamburg reached the European Cup Final while he was there only to lose to Nottingham Forest. He returned to England, who capped him 63 times, playing and managing at the highest level, though ironically it was after defeat by Germany at Wembley that he decided to resign as the National Manager.

FACTS & FIGURES

1. Most national teams play in colors that reflect their national flag, but there are two major exceptions amongst the European elite. The Netherland plays in its famous orange, while the Dutch flag is red, white, and blue. Italy's flag is green, red, and white, yet the team is nicknamed the "Azzurri" because of its blue shirts.

2. Benfica won successive European Finals in 1961 and 1962 but has subsequently lost in all its five finals since.

3. Cesare Maldini's son, Paolo, had an even more distinguished career than his father, playing professionally into his 40s and winning 23 trophies with AC Milan.

4. Liverpool won the European Cup four times between 1977 and 1984. Full back Phil Neal was the only player to appear in all four finals.

5. Howard Kendall was the youngest player to play in an FA Cup final when he played as a 17-year-old for Preston North End in its defeat against West Ham United. He went on to play for Everton to some effect and later managed the club to further success.

6. There was a maximum wage structure in England which

Newcastle's George Eastham decided to strike and refuse to play. It was £20, and Eastham wanted to move on to Arsenal, which he was able to do in 1963 when the structure and the transfer system as it existed was declared illegal in the High Court.

7. The Netherlands never lost a game when Johan Cruyff scored. That was in 33 of his 48 appearances.

8. Bill Nicholson signed Jimmy Greaves for Spurs in 1961 from AC Milan in a deal that was worked out by financial experts at the Treasury. The price was £99,999 in lira so that he didn't have the pressure of being the first £100,000 player.

9. Cruyff became a father just after his transfer to Barcelona in 1973 for 6 million guilders and gave him a Catalan name: Jordi.

10. Lev Yashin, the Russian goalkeeper who played in four World Cups, saved 151 penalties in his career and won the 1963 Ballon D'Or.

11. Franz Beckenbauer, the Bayern Munich and German captain when West Germany won the 1974 World Cup, was known as "The Kaiser" because of his authority on the ball.

12. Few remember much about Brazil in the 1966 World Cup except the team was subject to some rough play by Portugal and Bulgaria. Hungarians remember more because they simply outplayed the South Americans but went on to

lose in the quarter finals against Russia at Roker Park.

13. Rangers won the 1972 European Cup Winners Cup against Yashin's team, Moscow Dynamo, in Barcelona.

14. Sixteen months earlier at Ibrox in the Rangers Celtic Derby, 66 spectators died and many more were injured in a crush at a stairway.

15. Hosts Spain and then Italy won the European Nations Cup in 1964 and 1968, respectively, but the following two competitions saw away wins, Germany in Belgium in 1972, and Czechoslovakia in Yugoslavia in 1976.

16. Gerd Muller, who won the World Cup with Germany in 1974, scored an amazing 68 goals in 62 internationals and 365 goals for Bayern Munich in 427 games from 1964 until his final appearance in February 1979.

17. Laurent Pokou from the Ivory Coast won two Player of the Tournament titles at the African Nations Cup in 1968 and 1970, earning him comparison with Pele. He won every honor in the Ivory Coast before going to France to play for Nancy and Rennes.

18. Mali's Salif Keita was African Player of the Year in 1970, having won three successive league titles in France and the Portuguese Cup with Sporting.

19. Kazadi Mwamba had a difficult time in goal for Zaire in the 1974 World Cup, but he is generally regarded as one of the

best goalkeepers ever produced by Africa. He won the African Championships that year and previously in 1968, when he was voted Player of the Tournament.

20. Karim Abdul Razak from Ghana was a real globetrotter. He won African Player of the Year once and Player of the Tournament in 1978, when Ghana won its third African title while playing at different times in Egypt and the USA.

TRIVIA QUESTIONS

1. Who scored a hat-trick for England in the 1966 World Cup Final?

   A   Bobby Charlton

   B   Martin Peters

   C   Nobby Stiles

   D   Geoff Hurst

   E   Gordon Banks

2. Which German footballer scored more goals in internationals than the number of games he played?

   A   Paul Breitner

   B   Ged Muller

   C   Franz Beckenbauer

   D   Dieter Hoeness

   E   Franz Roth

3. Kevin Keegan left Liverpool for Germany. Which club did he join?

   A   Bayern Munich

   B   Borussia Monchengladbach

   C   Hamburg

   D   Stuttgart

E   Cologne

4. Who scored the winning goal in the 1973 FA Cup Final?

A   Ian Porterfield

B   Billy Hughes

C   Dave Watson

D   Jimmy Montgomery

E   Vic Halom

5. Portuguese Star Eusebio was born in which African country?

A   Zaire

B   Ghana

C   Mali

D   Ivory Coast

E   Mozambique

ANSWERS

1. D
2. B
3. C
4. A
5. E

CHAPTER 4

CHANGE, CONTROVERSY AND DISASTER

In many ways, the 1980s has been remembered for the problems in soccer rather than the high points. Loss of life is always tragic, and this period saw some incidents that are still reverberating years later. Many grounds were old and tired, and arguably not suitable for the matches they were hosting. Perhaps in the light of that, it was fortunate that there were not more problems. Soccer also seemed to become a means of expressing frustration with aspects of society. Without wanting to be controversial or political, there is no doubt that hooliganism found a vehicle in soccer which the authorities found hard to combat.

First Million Pound Player

Trevor Francis' move to Nottingham Forest in February 1979 has always been regarded as the first million-pound deal. Italy would dispute that and say that Giuseppe Savoldi moved from Bologna to Napoli for 2 billion lira which represented £1.2m. That deal was done in 1975, a couple of years after Johan Cruyff had gone from Ajax to Barcelona for the equivalent of £922,000. Whatever the rights and wrongs of this, there was no doubt that transfer fees were going up. Likewise, there was no doubt that Francis paid Forest back because he scored the only goal in the European Cup Final against Malmo.

In 1990, the record stood at £8m when Fiorentina sold Roberto Baggio to its close rival, Juventus. It was a time when Italian soccer was flourishing and money seemed no object. Money was to become a major talking point in the years that have followed since.

Brian Clough and Nottingham Forest

Brian Clough was a prodigious goal scorer for Middlesbrough then Sunderland, scoring an average of almost a goal a game, 251 in 274 league games, before an injury on Boxing Day at Roker Park against Bury in 1962 effectively ended his career. He became a manager when he was 30, at Fourth Division, Hartlepool, took Derby up from the Second Division, and then the First Division Championship and the semi-final of the European Cup where Derby lost to Juventus. He left and had a brief spell with Brighton before Leeds United came calling. He was the victim of player power lasting just a few weeks at Leeds United; how Leeds must regret that decision. He took over at Nottingham Forest, then mid-table in Division Two, and together with his friend Peter Taylor, whom he had known since his Middlesbrough days, won the First Division, followed by successive European Cups as well as four League Cups.

So how did he do it? He and Peter clearly had an eye for a player because the £1m purchase was a real exception. He gathered together players that some didn't want or who were yet to develop and molded them into a team.

John McGovern was a young winger whom he took with him everywhere and converted him into his midfield captain. Kenny Burns, Frank Clark, and Larry Lloyd were veteran defenders, while John Robertson no one seemed to want but was arguably his star even though Peter Shilton and Trevor Francis were probably the biggest names.

Liverpool was the holder of the European Cup when Forest first entered. There was no seeding, and the two met straight away. Most expected Liverpool to win, but Forest went through, winning the Cup against Malmo with that Francis goal. A year later, Hamburg was the runner-up with Forest scoring the only goal through Robertson at a game played at the Santiago Bernabeu in Madrid. Forest couldn't complete the treble, but next year there was still an English name on the Cup. The following season Liverpool won for a third time.

Aston Villa

Aston Villa won six domestic league titles by 1902 and has only managed one since, but it also led to its winning the European Cup at the first attempt. As a result, the Cup headed back to

England once again, moving down from the North West of England to the Midlands.

When Aston Villa won the English First Division title in 1980/1, it was as big a shock as Nottingham Forest's recent success. Ron Saunders had Ipswich as Villa's main rivals with more glamorous clubs trailing behind, including the current European Cup champions, Liverpool, as he finally managed Aston Villa to a first title in many decades. When the later stages of the European Cup campaign began, there was a new manager, Tony Barton.

It was to be the sixth year in a row that the Cup went to England. Holders, Liverpool went out at the quarter final stage.

Villa had beaten Valur, Berlin, only on away goals and Dynamo Kiev before facing Anderlecht in the semi-final. After a 1 – 0 win in the first leg at Villa Park, the English champions managed a 0 – 0 draw in Belgium to qualify for the Final against Bayern Munich.

In the final itself, Villa had some problems when its goalkeeper Peter Rimmer had to be replaced after ten minutes by Nigel Spink who had only played one senior game. He had a great game against a potent attack and kept a clean sheet.

The winner came in the 66th minute from center-forward Peter Withe after Villa had certainly to withstand pressure. It continued after the goal, but withstand it Villa did.

The team that made history for Villa that night in Rotterdam reads:

Rimmer (rep. Spink 10), Swain, Williams, Evans, McNaught, Mortimer, Bremner, Shaw, Withe, Cowans, Morley.

Aberdeen

Alex Ferguson had a fairly undistinguished playing career, yet in management has ensured his name will never be forgotten. His time at Manchester United will be discussed later, but his real success began at Aberdeen in the 1980s. It is a challenge in itself to take on the two Glasgow Clubs, Rangers and Celtic, but to take on Europe and win was astonishing.

Aberdeen took 12,000 fans to Gothenburg to watch it play Real Madrid in the final of the European Cup Winners' Cup in 1983. Rangers had won this Cup the previous year, while Celtic won the European Cup itself in 1967.

Ferguson had been just 36 when he arrived from St. Mirren in 1978, and together with Archie Knox made a formidable partnership. Aberdeen won the League two years later and the Cup in 1982. In the quarter finals of the Cup Winners Cup after drawing 0 – 0 with Bayern Munich, Aberdeen won the home leg 3 – 2. In contrast, Watershei of Belgium in the Semis was an easy task.

Aberdeen led in the final through Eric Black before conceding a penalty and the equalizer. John Hewitt headed home in extra time, and the Cup was to return to Scotland.

It is worth remembering the team that played that night: Jim

Leighton, John McMaster, Dug Rougvie, Willie Miller, Alex McLeish, Neale Cooper, Peter Weir, Gordon Strachan, Neil Simpson, Mark McGhee, Eric Black, Sub – John Hewitt.

Michel Platini

When discussions take place about the best French footballer of all time, fans of Manchester United are likely to claim it was Eric Cantona. He certainly made an impact for United after so many lean years, but that is all. Arsenal fans have a point when they say Thierry Henry, while Zinedine Zidane must certainly be considered. One player who certainly has a case that will be supported by every Juventus fan is Michel Platini. Recent publicity about Platini concerns UEFA, FIFA, and the issues of soccer corruption, and that is for a later chapter. For now, here is the case for Michel Platini.

He began his career at Nancy as a 17-year-old before going on to St. Etienne in 1979. It was his move to Juventus in 1982 that really brought him into the spotlight. He stayed until 1987, during which time Juventus won its first European Cup.

Nancy had won the French Ligue I while he was there, and St. Etienne won in 1981. Juventus reached the European Final in 1983, as well as winning the Intercontinental Cup. In 1984, Juventus won three trophies, the UEFA Super Cup, the Cup Winners Cup and the Italian League before finally taking the European Cup in 1985. During that period, Platini won what is commonly known as the

Ballon D'Or on three successive occasions.

He was also captaining France, with the Nation reaching the last four in both the 1982 and 1986 World Cups. In between, his 9 goals in 5 games helped France to become European Champions.

His record in 72 international games was 41 goals, while in Club soccer, he scored 224 goals in 432 games, 68 of those goals being for Juventus in 147 league games.

Liverpool and Heysel

In 1985, at the Heysel Stadium in Brussels, Liverpool lined up against Juventus trying to win its fourth European Cup in less than a decade. What was to happen off the pitch completely overshadowed the fact that Juventus went on to win the game.

With hindsight, it is easy to say that many soccer stadiums were dated and in need of modernization. That is only part of the story however.

Thirty-nine fans died that evening having arrived in the expectation of seeing a great game. They were crushed or suffocated to death. Whatever the blame, and it has been laid at more than one door, it was a tragedy that can never be forgotten. With the bodies still just outside the ground, the authorities decided that the game should go ahead with the justification that there was a huge crowd expecting a game. Chaos would result if it was canceled was the feeble claim.

There had been exuberance in the city during the day, but no more. However, there had been no action to prevent people with no tickets from traveling, and with the increased consumption of alcohol, there was damage in the city and the mood seemed to change.

There was no real segregation in the ground, and Juventus fans had been able to buy unsold tickets in the Liverpool end that had been returned by Liverpool. The result was a fairly tight area of Liverpool fans with its area reduced and more space for those of Juventus. In addition, some Liverpool fans knocked down a wall to get into that tight area which was clearly too full. They broke out and Juventus fans fled, but there was a retaining wall stopping them going too far. The result was a crush before a wall collapsed causing even more problems.

The game started at 9.41pm with Michel Platini scoring the only goal from a penalty. The game and the result were fairly irrelevant with Platini's celebration instinctive but inappropriate. The lap of honor defied belief.

One outcome was the English sides were banned from European competition for five years, but the whole episode remains very unsavory with several aspects very disturbing.

Maradona

Diego Maradona was still a teenager when Argentina won its first World Cup in 1978. His first trip abroad for senior soccer was to the Maracanã Stadium in Rio de Janeiro in 1979, where he played for an Argentina XI against a Brazil XI in an electric atmosphere. He soon emerged as a real star and is still hero-worshipped in Napoli where he played some of his best club soccer.

Starting his career at Argentinos, Maradona moved to Boca Juniors in Buenos Aires in July 1981, winning the league title in his only season before moving on to Barcelona. However, it was at Napoli in Italy that he spent his best days. Barcelona had bought him for a record fee and after two seasons made a good profit from the deal. He played at Napoli until the 1992/3 season when he had a single season at Sevilla before returning to play in Argentina until his ultimate retirement in 1997.

His international career deserves an article of its own, so here is the detail of his club years.

Bearing in mind he was an attacking midfielder rather than a striker, as such his return of 135 goals in 290 games was excellent, with 81 goals in 184 league games for Napoli. He had won the Spanish Cup and the Spanish Super Cup while at Barcelona. He went on to win Serie A twice, the Italian Cup, and Super Cup as well as the UEFA Cup with Napoli.

The Hand of God

Argentina won the World Cup for the second time in 1986 in Mexico. For some, it will always be remembered for the quarter final game between Argentina and England, and specifically Maradona's two goals, than for the final itself.

Maradona was awarded Argentina's first goal with a "header", having apparently beaten the England goalkeeper, Peter Shilton, in the air. Maradona is just 1.67 meters, much shorter than Shilton, so how did he do it? The answer was clearly shown afterwards and frankly should have been obvious to the referee, Ali Bin Nasser. Maradona jumped, stretched his arm up, and punched the ball over Shilton.

Maradona's second from halfway took him past several floundering Englishmen before he side-footed past Shilton into the English net, but the first still causes fury among the English. Antonio Rattin, the Argentina captain who was sent off against England twenty years earlier, would have had a wry smile on his face as it went in.

It was Maradona's second World Cup, and he was arguably in his prime and certainly more settled in his life than he had been since starting his football career.

After a goalless first half, Argentina had more of the ball but England the best chance. However, Argentina then took control with those two goals. Gary Lineker got a late consolation, but Argentina went through.

After the game, it was Maradona who gave the goal its now commonly used name: "a little with the head of Maradona and a little with the hand of God". He went on to score both goals in the 2 – 0 win over Belgium in the semi-final with West Germany, beating France by the same margin to set up a final between two previous winners.

Maradona was well marked in the final but goals from Jose Luis Brown and Valdano made it 2 – 0, but back came Germany. Scores were level after goals by Karl-Heinz Rummenigge and Rudi Voller. Back game Argentina with injury time looming and Maradona threaded a ball through to Jorge Burruchaga for the winner.

African Awakening

The relative success of Cameroon in the 1982 and 1990 World Cups gave impetus to African soccer. In 1982, it did not lose but was still eliminated on a tie-break of goals scored having been level with Italy in the Group. In 1986, it reached the quarter final only to lose to England by the margin of 3 – 2. "The Indomitable Lions" was the nickname of the side. It had won the African Nations Cup in 1984, beating Nigeria 3 – 1 in the final, lost on penalties to Egypt two years later after a 0 – 0 draw, before regaining the Trophy in 1988, once again beating its bigger neighbor Nigeria 1 – 0. In general, West African sides were the most consistent during that period with Ivory Coast and Ghana always putting out strong sides, even if Egypt was always a side to fear.

Russia Hides the Truth?

On 22nd October 1982, tragedy struck in Moscow. Although the official figures released by Izvestia, the Russian Government newspaper, said that 66 soccer fans were crushed to death one night, other sources put the figure as well above 300. It happened as they tried to go back into the stadium when there was a last-minute goal in the UEFA Cup tie between Moscow Spartak and the Dutch side, Haarlem.

Winter had come early, and the steps in the Lenin Stadium were treacherous. Because there was a small crowd of around 15,000, they were crammed into just part of the stadium that had hosted the Olympics and held over 100,000.

As fans left but then returned as Spartak scored again, they were trapped inside dark tunnels faced by others who were still leaving. The ice did the rest as fans slipped and were trampled.

There was a mass funeral and no real news coverage for weeks. No one blamed the militia, whom eye-witnesses had accused of adding to the problems, and the trial of the stadium chief who was made the scapegoat was not reported at all for years. He served 18 months corrective labor.

It was not until the end of the decade that the facts became clearer; that it had been the worst disaster in the history of soccer.

Asia

It was the Middle East sides that had success in the Asian Cup in the 1980s. Korea had won the first two trophies before Iran's dominance with three successive wins from 1968 through to 1976. Kuwait beat the Koreans in 1980 before two Saudi Arabia successes, the first against China and the second, in 1988, against South Korea again.

Soccer had been introduced into Asia by Europeans, but until the 80s, it had not really been embraced by the locals. The fact that China, with its vast population, reached the 1984 final was a good sign, but there was no sign of India, the other huge Asian country; it preferred another sport introduced from Europe, cricket.

Marco van Basten

Marco van Basten began his career as a teenager at UVV Utrecht before quickly moving to Ajax, and it was soon evident that this striker was special. He stayed for six seasons and won the Cup Winners' Cup with Ajax before the Italian Club AC Milan came calling, and he played the rest of his career there. At AC Milan, he joined Ruud Gullit and Frank Rijkaard; Italian money talked. His international record for the Netherlands was 24 goals in 58 games including 5 in 1988 when the Netherlands became European Champions.

He was only 28 when injury forced him to retire, but the preceding years were ones where spectators watched someone that was really special. He was another with three Ballon D'Ors—1988, 1989, and 1992—just before injury resulted in two years on the sidelines and his ultimate retirement.

Milan won the European Cup in 1989 and 1990. During van Basten's time in the side, Milan's roll of honour was:

Four Serie A titles, four Italian Cup, two European Cup, two Intercontinental Cup, two Super Cup.

He scored 276 goals in 376 games, 124 of those goals being for Juventus in 201 games. His Ajax record was even more impressive with 128 goals in 133 games.

North American Soccer League

The North American Soccer League finally collapsed in March 1985. Club soccer in North America had been tried, and at times it was very successful. In the 70s, several international stars, albeit basically at the end of their careers, had attracted good crowds. The signing of Pele created huge interest. New York Cosmos could get 70,000 watching its games when players like Beckenbauer, Cruyff, Best, and Eusebio were around, but there was no stable base. The league actually expanded to twenty-four teams in 1978, but as costs rose, franchises closed down. In just four years, seventeen had folded, so the end was inevitable.

The USA had always been seen as a country with great potential, even though it had popular sports that were already attracting large crowds. To date, that potential was still unfulfilled.

Hillsborough

Just four years after Heysel, there was an even worse disaster with 96 Liverpool fans killed in the Leppings Lane end of Hillsborough, Sheffield on 15th April 1959 as the FA Cup semi-final between Liverpool and Nottingham Forest was starting. For years afterwards, the POLICE laid the blame firmly at the door of the fans, but that has been reversed in recent inquests with charges now being levied at the police themselves.

"Unlawful killing" is the final verdict because the police have had to admit that they asked for an exit gate to be opened in the hope of easing the bottleneck that was developing. All it did was get more fans into a confined space with some actually dying from asphyxiation while standing up.

Attempts to get out of pens onto the side of the pitch failed, and fans simply had nowhere to go. The game was halted at 3.05pm, but by then there was little that could be done, and the problems were further exacerbated by a police cordon that prevented all but one of 44 ambulances to get into the stadium.

Crush barriers collapsed; the ground with hindsight was no longer suitable for huge crowds, and the authorities in general were ill-prepared for such an emergency.

Gazza and 1990

Although Argentina managed to reach the final of the next

World Cup in Italy in 1990, it was unable to retain the trophy, losing 1 – 0 to a late penalty from West Germany's Andreas Brehme. It had also needed penalties in the semi-final where it had beaten England on penalties after extra time. That game is remembered by English fans for the tears in Paul (Gazza) Gascoigne's eyes after being booked, because he realized that if England reached the final, he would be suspended for the game.

By now the World Cup was a truly global affair. Among the 24 nations competing in six groups of four were the UAE, Korea, Costa Rica, USA, Egypt, and Cameroon. Cameroon actually won its group and went through its first knockout stage game only to lose 3 – 2 to England in the quarter finals. Brazil actually lost to Argentina in the round of the last 16.

The semi-finalists were all past winners, the hosts Italy, the holders, Argentina, West Germany and England. Both semi-finals finished 1 – 1 after extra time and had to be decided on penalties.

FACTS & FIGURES

1. Valley Parade, the home of Bradford City, had an old wooden stand, and one fateful day in 1985, the rubbish that accumulated below it caught fire. Fans were trapped in the stand as the fire spread and 56 fans died.

2. It might be difficult to believe, but crowds in England were very poor at times in the 80s. Here are attendance figures from a weekend from February 1986. Arsenal 22,473, Manchester City 20,540, Chelsea 12,372, and Aston Villa 8,456, who were rewarded with a 0 – 0 against Southampton. The highest figure that weekend Everton against Tottenham, 33,178.

3. Kenny Dalglish, Liverpool player and manager, attended the funerals of all 96 fans who died at Hillsborough.

4. Everton won the League and European Cup Winners Cup in 1984/5 season, but the Heysel disaster meant it could not enter the European Cup itself the next year.

5. Despite dominating La Liga in the 1980s, Real Madrid was unable to add to its tally of European Cup wins.

6. Brazil's record in the World Cup through the 80s was poor, despite having the services of stars such as Zico and

Socrates.

7. The University of North Carolina, coached by Anson Dorrance, dominated the women's college game in the USA, winning sixteen of the first twenty NCAA championships, including nine between 1986 and 1994.

8. Turkey struggled in the 1980s; it conceded eight goals on three occasions, once against Poland and twice against England.

9. The Australian Football League was restricted to the East Coast of Australian after its formation in 1977 through the next two decades.

10. Jean Tigana was a vital member of the French side that became European Champions in 1984; he played 52 times in all for his country. He played in France throughout his career, starting at Cassis Carnoux and finally retiring with Marseille, winning Ligue 1 once and the French Cup twice.

11. One of the goals of the 1980s was scored by Argentinian Ricky Villa to win the FA Cup Final replay for Tottenham against Manchester City in 1981.

12. Keith Houchen's brilliant headed goal in Coventry City's 3 – 2 win over Tottenham in the 1987 FA Cup helped clinch the Midland's side the only trophy in its history.

13. PSV Eindhoven won the European Cup in 1988, going through on the away goal rule four times and then beating

Benfica on penalties in the Final.

14. The Brazilian side, Flamengo, based in Rio de Janeiro, won the Copa Libertadores then easily defeated Liverpool 3 – 0 in the Intercontinental Cup. This 1981 side is commonly regarded as the best Brazil has seen.

15. Igor Belanov scored a stunning hat-trick for the USSR against Belgium in the 1986 World Cup but still finished on the losing side; Belgium scored four in a game that went to extra time.

16. France beat Brazil 4 – 3 on penalties after a 1 – 1 draw to progress to the next stage of the 1986 World Cup. Zico scored his penalty in the shootout but missed one in real time that may have taken Brazil through.

17. In the previous World Cup, France had lost on penalties 5 – 4 against West Germany after a 3 – 3 draw.

18. Several outstanding players never managed to play in the pinnacle of the game—the World Cup. One who stands out in the 80s is the prolific Liverpool and Wales forward, Ian Rush.

19. Berndt Schuster was in the German side that won the European Championships, but he fell out with the management and retired from international soccer at 24. He made do with club success with Barcelona and Real Madrid instead.

20. By the time Northern Ireland finally reached the World Cup Finals in 1982, arguably its best ever player, George Best, had retired. Norman Whiteside was even younger than Pele when he made his debut in the World Cup, while the Irish caused a real shock by beating Spain in the early stages.

TRIVIA QUESTIONS

1. Which African nation was the first to reach a World Cup quarter final?

    A   Egypt

    B   Cameroon

    C   Ghana

    D   Ivory Coast

    E   Nigeria

2. Whom did Nottingham Forest beat to win its First European Cup?

    A   Liverpool

    B   Club Brugge

    C   Malmo

    D   Hamburg

    E   Real Madrid

3. Which Asian country lost in two Asian Cup Finals in the 1980s?

    A   South Korea

    B   Saudi Arabia

    C   China

    D   Kuwait

E   Iran

4. Where did Maradona have his greatest club success?

   A   Boca Juniors

   B   Sevilla

   C   Barcelona

   D   Argentinos

   E   Napoli

5. For whom was Michel Platini playing when he won his 3 Ballon D'Ors?

   A   St. Etienne

   B   Nancy

   C   AC Milan

   D   Juventus

   E   Sevilla

ANSWERS

1. B
2. C
3. A
4. E
5. D

CHAPTER 5
A Truly Global Game

By the 1990s, there were few parts of the world where soccer was not popular, although it didn't necessarily mean it was always the main sport. There was considerable change on the way with players soon being able to take far more control over their playing futures. Similarly, the soccer calendar, especially in Europe, was to become even busier with competitions expanding and the financial rewards for success growing accordingly.

The Formation of the Premier League

Leeds United's First Division title in 1991/2 was the end of an era. The following season saw the launch of the Premier League that over the next years became the most popular and best-financed league in the world with matches eventually beamed across every time zone.

Initially, it still had twenty-two teams, but since 1995, that number was reduced to twenty, created by relegating four clubs and promoting just two. Seventy-two Football League clubs were thus equally divided into three Leagues of twenty-four.

The promotion-relegation link between the top Football League Division (the Championship) and the Premiership has always been in place. Three up, three down has been the system since 1995, although promotion for the third club is via a playoff system. UEFA has subsequently sought a limit of eighteen teams for each top division, but the Premiership rejected that, and the debate has gone away.

The twenty-two clubs that formed the first Premier League in alphabetical order were Arsenal, Aston Villa, Blackburn Rovers, Chelsea, Coventry City, Crystal Palace, Everton, Ipswich Town, Leeds United, Liverpool, Manchester City, Manchester United, Middlesbrough, Norwich City, Nottingham Forest, Oldham Athletic, Queens Park Rangers, Sheffield United, Sheffield Wednesday, Southampton, Tottenham Hotspur, and Wimbledon.

Luton and Notts County were two of the clubs that agreed to the formation of the Premiership, but they were relegated just before its introduction.

The logic for the "break" was in order to take advantage of the sponsorship and television deals that were anticipated. Carling was the first title sponsor, maintaining its sponsorship until 2001. Sky won the rights to televise games, and that has also proved to be extremely profitable.

Just eleven " foreign players" from outside the UK and Ireland were playing in the English top division at the time. By the millennium, 36% of the players were "foreign." Indeed, Chelsea fielded a team where all the team were foreign in 1999.

In terms of transfer fees, Alan Shearer's move to Blackburn from Southampton exceeded £3m, a record, but after winning the Title at Blackburn, he moved on to his "hometown" Newcastle for £15m in 1996.

Denmark Springs a Surprise

Denmark has never been one of the giants of the European game though it has produced a number of good players over the years. The highlight of its soccer history is undoubtedly its winning of the 1992 European Championships held in Sweden. It had only had a week to prepare the squad when the invitation came to compete after Yugoslavia, in a state of war, was not allowed to participate.

Qualifiers had to win through their groups over the two years preceding the final with two groups playing in the final stages to provide four semi-finalists.

In Group 1, the successful teams were Sweden, the hosts, and Denmark with France and England being eliminated. In Group 2, Scotland and the Commonwealth of Independent States (a transitional side as the USSR was breaking up) went home as Germany and the Netherlands progressed.

In the semi-finals, Denmark defeated the Netherlands 5 – 4 on penalties after a 2 – 2 draw, while Germany guaranteed no home success by beating Sweden 3 – 2. The stage was set for

Germany, a country with a great international record, to play a relative "minnow", Denmark, in Gothenburg on 26th June.

Goals by John Jensen and Kim Vilfort supported by a great goalkeeper, Peter Schmeichel, gave Denmark a surprising 2 – 0 victory.

The Bosman Ruling and its Implications

The face of soccer changed dramatically in 1995, when a court ruling resulted in players being able to take charge of their own affairs like never before. A journeyman professional, Jean-Marc Bosman played in midfield for RFC Liege in Belgium in 1990 but wanted to move on. There was an offer from Dunkirk in France, and his contract was coming to an end. The problem was that the clubs could not agree on a fee, so Bosman was stuck; Dunkirk's offer was withdrawn because it refused the £250,000 transfer fee, and Liege then slashed his wages by 75%, so Bosman was trapped.

He went to a lawyer called Jean-Louis Dupont who tried to resolve Bosman's problems, expecting it could be done quickly. No one took the issue seriously. The case went to court and Bosman had his freedom, but it was now 1995, and Bosman had spent two years living in his garage. It was a hollow victory, but the implications of the case were far-reaching.

Players who were out of contract could leave their existing clubs without any transfer fee being due; freedom of movement was guaranteed within the EU. Players could negotiate better contracts where an interested club had no transfer fee to pay. A couple of examples of events in England are Blackburn Rovers paying Chris Sutton £10,000-a-week footballer in 1994 and 2001, and Sol Campbell getting £100,000-a-week to go to Arsenal from Tottenham.

When you add agents to the mix, the whole face of soccer changed, even if Bosman himself didn't benefit from the judgment.

The USA Hosts the World Cup

Soccer broke new ground in 1994. To date, the competition had always taken place in either Europe or South America. It was a real statement of intent to award the Cup to USA where the game was far from being the most popular sport on the Continent—or even the second or third most popular. There was no existing national soccer league, so it was a slight risk, but it was the most profitable to date, played in nine cities across this huge country.

Saudi Arabia actually won two games within its Group, 2 – 1 against Morocco and 1 – 0 over Belgium, but it was Belgium that went through to the last 16. It did better than the hosts who, although the USA beat Colombia 2 – 1, lost by a single goal to Romania and Brazil.

Bulgaria reached the semi-finals, having beaten Germany the

round before. It was joined by Sweden, but the two sides were both defeated at that stage, Italy beating Bulgaria 2 – 1 and Brazil beating Sweden by a single goal. Sweden easily won the third-place playoff, but the final in the Los Angeles Rose Bowl was scoreless and had to be decided on penalties with Brazil prevailing.

A French First

When the 1998 World Cup went to France, there had been six previous winners, three from Europe and three from South America. Of those six, five had won on foreign soil with England only succeeding at home. In most cases, the home nation was usually among the favorites, so France appeared to be in with a good chance of becoming the seventh name to be put on the Jules Rimet Trophy.

South Africa made its first appearance in the World Cup Finals and managed two draws in its three games. Nelson Mandela's release early in the decade gave impetus to every sector of national life, although the South Africans could not get past the group stage. Another African country, Nigeria, actually won its group but was soundly beaten 4 – 1 by Denmark in the last 16.

Japan and Jamaica both found themselves in a difficult group. Argentina had been a real world power for years, and while Croatia was a small and relatively new country, plenty of talented players had been produced by this part of what was formerly Yugoslavia. The USA qualified again but returned home pointless with Iran the other non-qualifier from that Group.

Argentina and England drew 2 – 2 in the first knockout stage, but it was Argentina who prevailed on penalties only to fall 2 – 1 to the Dutch in the quarter finals. The hosts, France, was only able to get beyond the quarter finals by winning against Italy on penalties after a 0 – 0 draw. Croatia's 3 – 0 win over Germany was definitely one of the results of the whole competition.

France found its form in the semi-finals, beating Croatia 2 – 1, while Brazil beat the Netherlands on penalties after a 1 – 1 draw. There was no such doubt in the final, but it was France that won easily 3 – 0. Zinedine Zidane scored twice in the first half, and the Emmanuel Petit injury-time third was icing on the cake.

Japan & South Korea

Four years later, it was off to Asia for the first time with the Cup held in South Korea and Japan. Japan had lost all three games in France but was certainly looking forward to hosting the competition jointly with its neighbor. The final was scheduled for Tokyo incidentally.

There were thirty-two teams playing in eight groups of four, and a few countries enjoyed real success for the first time. In Group A, Denmark and Senegal, went through with two former winners eliminated, Uruguay and France, that only got a single point.

China played in Group C, but it was Brazil and Turkey who went forward.

Korea and the USA went through at the expense of Poland and Portugal, with Argentina also failing behind Sweden and England. Japan won Group H, so both the hosts safely reached the next stage.

This was the first time a "Golden Goal" was used as opposed to playing a set period of extra time and Senegal benefitted from this change, reaching the quarter finals by beating Sweden 2 – 1. There were no goals in the Spain/Republic of Ireland game, so penalties were used, with Spain going through. The USA beat Mexico, with the other standout score, Korea beating Italy 2 – 1. The other hosts were beaten however, Japan losing by the single goal to Turkey.

Turkey beat Senegal with that valuable "Golden Goal", and Korea beat Spain on penalties. The other two semi-finalists were regulars; Brazil who beat England 2 – 1, and Germany, winners 1 – 0 over the USA. Two dreams died in the semi-finals; Germany beat Korea 1 – 0 in Seoul while Germany won by a similar score against Turkey. The latter won the third-place playoff for its best ever World Cup finish; indeed, Korea achieved that as well.

In the final, Brazil took the Cup in Yokohama with two goals from Ronaldo who thereby made up for his disappointment four years earlier.

Sir Alex Ferguson

Alex Ferguson was born in Govan, Glasgow, on the last day of 1941. His soccer playing career was nothing special. He began at Queen's Park as a 16-year-old amateur while working in the shipyards. He turned professional with Dunfermline in 1964 and scored 31 goals that season, enough to persuade Rangers to buy him for £65,000. The move was not a great success, and after two more moves, he retired in 1974.

East Stirlingshire took him on as manager almost immediately, but he soon moved on to St. Mirren with whom he won the league. In 1978, he became manager of Aberdeen, and during his time, he won three league titles, four Scottish Cups, as well as the European Cup Winners Cup. He was seen as the man to revive Manchester United, where he went in November 1986. He managed to get United to second in one of his first four seasons, but generally United were offering mid-table soccer. He was less than secure in the job, but winning the FA Cup in 1989/90 helped to give him some breathing space. Everyone at United will look back and be delighted that he stayed.

The Premier League was about to start, and in its first eleven seasons, 1992-3 to 2002-3, United won the title on an unprecedented eight occasions. In addition, United won the FA Cup a further three times with the 1998/9 season being the highlight with a domestic double and the Champions League. United was under pressure against Bayern Munich for most of the game, but two injury-time goals from substitutes Teddy Sheringham and Ole Gunnar Solskjaer changed a losing position, one down, into an astonishing success.

Ferguson was knighted in 1999, but he wasn't done yet. He added five more Premier League titles, a further Champions League success, and an FA Cup before retiring at the end of the 2012/3 season.

He was Manager of the Year a record eleven times and remains a board member and club ambassador since his retirement. Manchester United has not won the Premiership title since he retired.

The Class of '92

With transfer fees and costs in general rising, it became increasingly important for clubs to develop their own talent. While Manchester United had always been one of the wealthiest clubs around, it could not have imagined what an astonishing wealth of talent it had in a single youth side in 1992. Alan Hansen, the Liverpool and Scotland center-back, was famous for saying that no one wins anything with kids. The "kids" in the "Class of '92" proved him to be wrong as they came through to senior football. They joined a driving force in Roy Keane, the enigmatic Eric Cantona, and the stage was set for an astonishing period in English football. All have now retired, but here is a summary of the careers of those who had successful careers at Manchester United. (Incidentally, others in that youth side, notably Keith Gillespie and Robbie Savage, also had successful Premier League careers elsewhere as well as a significant number of international appearances for Northern Ireland and Wales respectively.)

David Beckham: Manchester United 1993 – 2003, 394 appearances and 85 goals, 6 PL titles, Champions League, 2 FA Cups, Intercontinental Cup. Real Madrid 2003 – 7. 155 appearances, 20 goals, La Liga and Spanish Super Cup. He had a successful MLS career with LA Galaxy as well as short loan periods at AC Milan with a Serie A success, and Paris St. Germain. He played 115 times for England, 57 as captain and scored 17 goals.

Ryan Giggs: Manchester United 1990 – 2014, 963 appearances and 168 goals, all at Manchester United. 13 PL titles, 2 Champions League, 4 FA Cups, 3 League Cups, Intercontinental Cup, UEFA Super Cup, Club World Cup. He played 64 times for Wales, scoring 12 goals.

Gary Neville: Manchester United 1994 – 2011, 592 appearances and 7 goals all at Manchester United. 10 PL titles, 2 Champions League, 3 FA Cup, 3 League Cup. World Club Cup. 85 England caps.

Phil Neville: Manchester United 1994 – 2005, 669 appearances and 13 goals in senior club football. 6PL titles, Champions League, 3 FA Cups, Intercontinental Cup. Everton 2005 – 13. 59 caps for England.

Paul Scholes: Manchester United 1994 – 2013, 705 appearances and 149 goals all for Manchester United. 11 PL titles, 2 Champions League, 4 FA Cup, 3 League Cup, World Club Cup. 66 England caps with 14 goals.

Nicky Butt: Manchester United 1994 – 2004. 570 appearances and 33 goals in senior club football. 7PL titles, Champions League, 3 FA Cups, Intercontinental Cup. Birmingham City on loan. Newcastle United 2006 – 10. 39 England Caps.

George Weah

The first real African soccer superstar, certainly the one that made the greatest impact in Europe, was the Liberian George Weah, who incidentally is now the president of the country as of early 2018.

His best season was 1995, when he won the African, European, and World footballer titles in that single season.

In his European career, he played for many famous clubs— Monaco, Paris Saint-Germain, AC Milan, and Chelsea as a striker. Football dominated his early years to the neglect of education, but why wouldn't you concentrate on soccer when you clearly have such talent?

He was born in Liberia's capital Monrovia in a neighborhood that could accurately be described as a slum. He loved his soccer and began with the Cameroonian club Tonnerre Yaounde before heading for Europe and Monaco in 1988 for just £135,000. He did not play for the first six months but clearly had the determination to prove he was good enough to make an impact. Arsene Wenger was coach there at the time, and Weah had the utmost respect for the man whose time at Arsenal exceeds two decades.

He was African Footballer of the Year while at Monaco where he also won the French Cup, but his greatest success was at Paris St. Germain, who had bought him for £5.8m. While he was there, he won the League, the Cup twice, and the League Cup as well as two more African Footballer awards, the Ballon D'Or, and European titles.

When he moved on to AC Milan for £6.2m, he was part of the side that won 2 Serie A Titles, and finally in 2000, he won the FA Cup with Chelsea when on loan from Milan. He retired in 2003 after short spells with Manchester City, Marseille, and Al-Jazira.

He played 60 times for Liberia, scoring 23 goals.

Real Madrid Is Back

There was a time when the European Cup was synonymous with Real Madrid. After all, it won the first five Cups and a sixth shortly afterwards. However, that went back to the 60s, and further success proved fairly elusive. The 7th Cup win was not until the 1 – 0 success against Juventus in 1997/8. Eight and nine were to follow fairly quickly, a comprehensive win over fellow Spanish side, Valencia in the 1999/2000 season by 3 – 0 after

Valencia had comprehensively disposed of Barcelona in the two-legged semi-final. Bayer Leverkusen was the third club to lose to Real, beaten 2 – 1 in 2001/2 in Glasgow.

Real Madrid had always signed the best players available, and the sides that won these three Cups in such a short time included many household names. Raul, Roberto Carlos, and Clarence Seedorf were all in the side that beat Juventus in Amsterdam with Predag Mijatovic scoring the game's only goal in the 66th minute. Valencia fell foul of goals by Morientes, Raul, and McManaman in the Paris encounter.

Zinedine Zidane and Raul scored Real's two goals against the Germans. Roberto Carlos, Figo, Morientes, Salgado, and Makalele were just a few of the names in the Real starting lineup. Lucio had equalized Raul's early goal, but Zidane's second proved to be the winner.

Women's World Cup

FIFA introduced a Women's World Cup in 1991, the venue China, with Chinese Taipei, Nigeria, and New Zealand giving a real international flavor among the entrants. There were twelve sides in all, playing in three groups of four with eight qualifying for the knockout stage of quarter, semi, and final. The semi-finals were fairly one-sided affairs, USA beating Germany 5 – 2 and Norway beating Scandinavian neighbors, Sweden 4 – 1. The USA became the first World Champions, winning the Final 2 – 1.

Four years later, the Cup moved on to Sweden. It was used to decide qualifiers for the following year's Olympic Games as well as deciding the World Champions. This time, it was Norway who prevailed, beating Germany 2 – 0. China and the USA were the beaten semi-finalists, both losing 1 – 0.

In 1999, sixteen teams gathered in the USA, this time creating four groups of four. Among the new entrants were Australia and Ghana. The two finalists were the previous tournament's beaten semi-finalists, with USA beating China on penalties after a goalless stalemate.

The USA had been an unqualified success, so the Cup returned there in 2003, but there was no home winner. Australia competed for the first time, but the Cup returned to Europe with Germany, having fallen behind, coming back to beat the favorites, Sweden 2 – 1, with a golden goal.

The Demise of the European Cup Winners' Cup

The European Cup Winners' Cup had begun in 1961 with Fiorentina being the first name on the Cup. It lost in the final the following season, and that was to be a trend. No club was able to retain the trophy, which became increasingly irrelevant as attention was very much focussed on the main competition, the European Cup.

The English had enjoyed it, with its clubs winning it a total of eight times, with Spain and Italy both having seven successes. It fulfilled a role while it existed, but it was never a close competitor to the main competition.

The last season when the competition was run was the 1998/9 season with national cup winners subsequently entering the UEFA Cup unless they had already qualified for the enlarged Champions League, the new competition that UEFA had approved.

The Expansion of the Champions League

There was no doubt that the European Cup had been a great success, and as television and sponsorship opportunities in soccer were increasing, it was seen as a logical move to revise the competition. The Champion Club from each league was eligible together with the previous season's winners if it had not won its own league.

The revised arrangements created a much-expanded competition.

The name change was in 1992/3 season, but the structure change in 1997 was quite dramatic. Instead of the competition where clubs had to win their domestic competition in order to qualify, multiple clubs from the major leagues were able to enter. It was an answer for the traditionally stronger clubs that may draw an equally strong side in the first round of a knockout competition and go no further.

Initially, league runners-up could play, and two years later, a further expansion meant that some leagues could provide four teams. In some circumstances, such as when the holder did not qualify from its league position, there could even be five. That represented at least 25% of a single league.

It pandered to sponsors, television, and the strong clubs of Europe, and still does.

Winners of smaller European Leagues found themselves in a series of preliminary leagues in order to get to the main competition where a large league had three teams waiting and a fourth as possible qualifying opposition for them. They had to start several weeks before the soccer season started in earnest, facing quite a task to make the competition proper.

The chances of a giant-killing act had virtually disappeared overnight. The competition proper involved leagues with teams playing on a home and away basis. At times, a fancied team did not go through, but even then, as long as it finished third of four it got another chance in the secondary European competition at an advanced stage.

Suddenly, the trophy cabinet appeared to be less important than qualifying for the Champions League; it became all about money, you see! Since this new system was introduced, the following teams were not their domestic champions when the won the Champions League, covering eighteen seasons:

Real Madrid (4), Barcelona (2), AC Milan (2), Chelsea (1), Bayern

Munich (1), Liverpool (1).

No current holder of its domestic league has won the Champions League since Barcelona in 2010/1, six seasons at the time of writing.

The Inaugural World Club Championship

January 2000, in Brazil, saw a new competition introduced to find a World Club Champion rather than just have the Intercontinental Cup game between the European Champions and the South American Champions. Eight teams were invited to play in two groups of four.

Group A comprised Real Madrid from Spain, Raja Club Athletic from Morocco, Sport Club Corinthians Paulista of Brazil, and Al Nazr of Egypt. It played its games in Sao Paulo. Group B was Manchester United, the current European Cup holders from England, South Melbourne from Australia, Vasco da Gama, also from Brazil, and Nexaca from Mexico, and the games were played in Rio de Janeiro.

Nexaca beat Real Madrid on penalties after a 1 − 1 draw to take third place with the final taking place immediately afterwards in the Maracanã Stadium. The final was between the two Brazilian sides with the Sao Paulo side, Corinthians, defeating the Rio side, Vasco da Gama.

Subsequently, a new competition has been devised, but it has yet to really capture the imagination of supporters beyond those whose teams are participating.

The Invincibles

While the story of the Premier League in England was largely a story of Manchester United until major investment created competition from Chelsea and latterly Manchester City, United had one major competitor, and that was Arsene Wenger's Arsenal. Arsenal has three Premiership titles to date with the third being part of a remarkable unbeaten run which began in May 2003 at the end of the 2002/3 season and went right through the 2003/4 season. It did not finish until towards the end of October in the 2004/5 season with a 2 – 0 defeat against Manchester United at Old Trafford. It is a record that is unlikely ever to be matched, although the previous record had been impressive as well; 42 games by Nottingham Forest between November 1977 and November 1978.

There had been one other instance of a side going through the whole season in the top flight undefeated, but that was Preston North End in 1988/9 when the season was only twenty-two games, not Arsenal's thirty-eight.

In the 2003/4 season, Arsenal scored in all but four games. However, the run began with the last two games of the previous season. The goals for and against columns were impressive with only 35 goals conceded against 112 scored. When the run finally ended, Arsenal had started the 2004/5 season with eight wins and a draw, but it was unable to retain the title, beaten by Chelsea who had been bought by a major investor—but more of that in the next chapter.

There was no doubt that nerves set in as Arsenal moved towards a complete undefeated season. It fell behind to already relegated Leicester City in the last game of the campaign before coming back to win 2 - 1. Despite being high scoring, these were the last few results: Arsenal 0 Birmingham 0, Portsmouth 1 Arsenal 1, Fulham 0 Arsenal 1, before the Leicester City game.

Thierry Henry missed just one of those 49 games, scoring 39 goals in the process. Robert Pires scored 23 goals from 40 starts and 5 substitute appearances. Kolo Toure and Jens Lehmann were the other two players to appear more than 40 times. With other players such as Patrick Viera, Sol Campbell, and Denis Bergkamp, Arsenal has a real quality squad that will never be forgotten.

FACTS & FIGURES

1. Blackburn Rovers, with the potent strike force of Alan Shearer and Chris Sutton, won the English Premier League in the 1994/5 season despite losing its last game at Anfield because West Ham held Manchester United to a draw at Upton Park. Liverpool legend Kenny Dalglish was the Blackburn manager, so in the end, everyone within Anfield was happy when the news of the draw came through.

2. La Liga had an unfamiliar look in 2000; Deportivo De La Coruna won the Title and Espanyol was runner-up. Other than in 1996, when Atletico Madrid won, it had been Barcelona or Real Madrid since 1985.

3. During the same period as Manchester United won those eight titles in eleven seasons, Bayern Munich won the Bundesliga six times. Unlike Manchester United, Bayern Munich continues to dominate its league.

4. The Japanese J League was the first time national soccer became fully professional. It began in 1993 with just ten teams. Previously, soccer had been played just by universities and company teams. The opening game was watched by an excited crowd of 60,000.

5. The release of Nelson Mandela gave real momentum to

South African soccer. The South African Football Association was founded in 1991, and South Africa successfully qualified for the 1998 and 2002 World Cups.

6. The USA celebrated being awarded the 1994 World Cup by qualifying for the previous competition in Italy for the first time in 40 years. To do so, it had to win in Trinidad & Tobago in front of a small but very excitable crowd in its last qualifying game.

7. The last ever FA Cup Final that went to a replay was in 1993, when Arsenal beat Sheffield Wednesday 2 – 1 in the second game after the first was drawn 1 – 1 after extra time.

8. Future England manager Sven-Goran Eriksson took SS Lazio to only its second-ever Serie A title in 1999 – 2000, its Centenary year. The team included Diego Simeone, Juan Sebastian Veron, Attilio Lombardo, Roberto Mancini and Fabrizio Ravanelli.

9. Olympique de Marseille won five successive Ligue 1 titles starting in 1988/9. In 1992/3, it also won the first "rebranded" Champions League defeating AC Milan 1 – 0 in the Final in Munich with a goal from Basile Boli. Marcel Desailly, Didier Deschamps, Rudi Voller, and Alen Boksic were the stars of that side. Bernard Tapie, its owner, was later charged with corruption and bribery relating to Marseille's domestic games.

10. In 2001, Michael Owen of Liverpool and England became the first English winner of the Ballon D'Or since two-time winner, Kevin Keegan, another Liverpool player but then at Hamburg, won in 1979.

11. Luis Figo, the Portuguese international, made the brave step to leave Barcelona for its fierce rivals Real Madrid in July 2000, the season he won the Ballon D'Or, for £54m. He stayed for five seasons before moving on to Inter. He also played 127 times for Portugal, scoring 32 goals.

12. Galatasary won the first European title for a Turkish Club when it won the UEFA Cup in 1999/2000 by defeating Arsenal on penalties.

13. The last decade of the 20th Century saw nine different winners of the Copa Libertadores in South America. Only Sao Paulo that won in successive seasons, 1992 and 1993, managed to get its name on the trophy twice.

14. Ajax won the 40th European Cup, now the Champions League, in 1995, and at the same time prevented AC Milan from getting a third successive win. Patrick Kluivert scored the only goal of the game.

15. Clarence Seedorf from that Ajax side left for Real Madrid after that win and subsequently played in Italy for AC Milan. He won three European titles with three different clubs, the only player currently to do so.

16. Edwin van der Sar was Ajax goalkeeper that night and went on to win the Cup a second time, playing for Manchester United in the all-English Final of 2008.

17. Euro 1996 was held in England, and the hosts once again lost on penalties to Germany 6 – 5 in the semi-finals after a 1 – 1 draw. England had come through the previous round against Spain, also on penalties after a goalless game. Germany took the Cup, beating Czechoslovakia 2 – 1 with a "Golden Goal," having beaten it 2 – 0 in an earlier qualifying game.

18. France followed up its World Cup win by becoming European Champions in 2000. It beat Italy, 2 – 1, in Rotterdam again with a "Golden Goal."

19. Joseph " Sepp" Blatter became the 8th President of FIFA in 1998, and his years of tenure ultimately caused huge controversy.

20. Liverpool has eighteen top flight titles but has yet the win the Premier League, which to date is 25 years old.

TRIVIA QUESTIONS

1. Name the footballer that has won the Champions League with three different clubs.

    A   Clarence Seedorf

    B   David Beckham

    C   Luis Figo

    D   Zinedine Zidane

    E   Patrick Kluivert

2. Which Europe country withdrew before the 1992 European Championships, with Denmark being asked to replace it?

    A   The Netherlands

    B   Germany

    C   Italy

    D   Yugoslavia

    E   England

3. How many times did Manchester United win the Premier League in its first eleven seasons?

    A   5

    B   7

    C   10

    D   4

E   8

4. Arsenal had a long unbeaten run in the English top flight. How many games was it?

    A   42
    B   49
    C   22
    D   38
    E   45

5. Who eliminated Germany from the World Cup in France in 1998?

    A   Italy
    B   Spain
    C   Croatia
    D   England
    E   Brazil

ANSWERS

1. A
2. D.
3. E
4. B
5. C

CHAPTER 6
HIGH FINANCE & A POWER STRUGGLE

Abramovich and Chelsea

When Russian oligarch Roman Abramovich came knocking on Chelsea's door, the face of English football changed forever. Chelsea's only first division title had been back in the 1950s. The club had had some success in Cups but had never shown the ability to challenge Manchester United, or indeed, Arsenal, in the modern era. Abramovich changed all that, and subsequent ownership changes have made the Premiership a home for a series of foreign investors.

Abramovich bought Chelsea from Ken Bates for £60m in July 2003. Few in the UK had heard of him, but in the first decade alone he was to spend £2 bn. In his first season, Chelsea was second under manager Claudio Ranieri, but that was not good enough. Ranieri was sacked and replaced by Jose Mourinho, a young Portuguese who had taken Porto to the Champions League title the previous season.

Chelsea immediately won a Premier League and League Cup

double, won the League again the following year, and the FA Cup and League Cup "double" the season after that. Avram Grant came in to replace Mourinho and almost achieved Abramovich's dream of the Champions League; Chelsea lost to Manchester United in a penalty shootout.

Over the years, managers have come and gone on a regular basis with five Premier League titles to date and that elusive Champions League win in 2001-2 under temporary manager Roberto di Matteo. The domestic Cup wins are almost incidental.

Star players have come and gone with Chelsea not bothering to match the huge transfer fees that have happened in the last couple of years. Fernando Torres is still the most expensive purchase at £50m from Liverpool in 2010-1. He was a relative failure, although he scored an important Champions League goal.

What Abramovich has spent is a fairly insignificant sum to him but an absolute fortune to average Premiership clubs who have seen the gap widen between top and bottom even though they are richly rewarded for being part of the League.

One Night in Istanbul

Liverpool is one of the clubs that has taken advantage of the expansion of the Champions League. It has rarely looked likely to win the English Premiership, but it has twice reached the Final in the 21st Century and on one night in Istanbul in 2005, there was a quite remarkable match. Liverpool had won the Cup four times at that point, but its opponent AC Milan had had six successes.

The night did not start well for Liverpool, as Milan's captain Paolo Maldini scored in the first minute. The Argentinian Hernan Crespo then scored twice just before halftime, so Liverpool looked out of it. However, led by its own captain, Steven Gerrard, Liverpool scored three times in eight minutes with Gerrard's header on 54 minutes being quickly followed by substitute Vladimir Smicer (56) and Xabi Alonso (60) getting Liverpool level.

There was to be no more scoring either in the final thirty minutes of normal time nor the thirty minutes of extra time. The Cup was therefore decided on penalties with AC Milan missing three of its attempts, Serginho, Pirlo, and Shevchenko, leaving Liverpool, with just a single miss from four penalties, winning without having to take the fifth. Incidentally, penalty scorers for Liverpool were Dietmar Hamann, Djibril Cisse, and Smicer.

It was a night of joy for Liverpool but devastation for AC Milan. However, two years later, AC Milan had revenge by beating a much-changed Liverpool 2 – 1 in a repeat in the 2007 Final in Athens. One thing hadn't changed; Maldini was still Milan captain, and this was his eighth final appearance.

Manchester City

The face of the Premiership continued to change, and arguably the purchase of Manchester City Sheikh Mansour Bin Zayed Al Nahyan and the Abu Dhabi United Group has had an even greater impact than Abramovich. City had been owned by Thaksin Shinawatra, the deposed Thai Prime Minster who faced corruption charges and had had his assets frozen. The result was that City was facing problems before the Abu Dhabi United Group came along.

In a decade, City has changed from an average side to one that can expect to be challenging for every trophy it enters. The resources were in place to sign top players, and although there has been quite a turnover in the team, there has been no doubting that Sheikh Mansour's investment has worked.

Near neighbors United suddenly found it had serious competition for the top talent. City won its first Premiership title in dramatic fashion in the 2011/2 season. United had already won 1 – 0 against Sunderland at the Stadium of Light and would be champions again if City failed to win. The City game had not finished, but United players and manager Sir Alex Ferguson thought they had done enough as they waited for the final whistle back in Manchester. Well into injury time, Sergio Aguero scored City's winner after it had trailed at the end of normal time against 10-man QPR that had already been relegated.

A second title came two years later with United winning in the intervening season. The recruitment of Pep Guardiola before the 2016/7 season was designed to add more titles as well as make a serious assault on the Champions League that has been going to Spain in recent seasons.

South Africa

FIFA broke new ground in 2010 by taking the World Cup to South Africa. The post-apartheid South Africa had successfully hosted the Rugby World Cup back in 1995, and this sports-mad country was delighted to take this even bigger competition. It was more than capable because the country had a good transport infrastructure, accommodation, and stadia.

It was disappointing that South Africa could not get out of its group, first and second going to Uruguay and Mexico. However, its 2 – 1 win over France and draw with Mexico in the opening match of the tournament in Johannesburg got them four points against just the one that France managed.

Argentina won its group with 100% record while USA beat England on goals scored as both went through. Germany and the Netherlands both won their groups, but another "giant", Italy, went out, finishing bottom of its Group with just two points. Paraguay and Slovakia went through from that group.

Both Korean sides had qualified, but just the Republic (South) made the knockout phase with Ghana the only African side from six to do so. Korea then lost, but Ghana continued along with, among others, Germany, who although it beat England 4 – 1, was extremely fortunate that there was no goal-line technology. Frank Lampard's shot, which should have been an equalizer for 2 – 2, was ruled out. Later, it was clear from film and photograph that the ball was well over the line. Ironic when the evidence from the

1966 World Cup Final had never been so clear.

Germany scored another 4 in beating Argentina while the Netherlands beat Brazil 2 – 1. There was more controversy when Ghana looked to have beaten Uruguay with a last-minute goal only for Luis Suarez to "play goalkeeper." He was sent off, but Ghana missed the penalty, the game was drawn, and the South Americans proceeded to the semis, without the suspended Suarez.

Spain was the other semi-finalist, beating Paraguay 1 – 0 and then Germany by the same score. The Netherlands beat Uruguay 3 – 2 but then produced a most disappointing and negative performance in the final. Every neutral was delighted that Spain won, again 1 – 0 with a goal from Iniesta as penalties loomed. Seven yellow cards, and a second, and therefore a red for John Heitinga reflected how the Netherlands played although Spain had five themselves.

Spain

One name missing on the Jules Rimet Trophy was Spain, that was until 2010 when it became the eighth name to be engraved on the trophy. Spain has had a proud history with a silver medal at the 1920 Olympics, fourth in the 1950 World Cup, the UEFA European Championship in 1964, runners-up twenty years later, and the Olympic gold medal in 1992. It was silver at the 2000 Olympics, but a golden period came with the 2008 UEFA

European Championship, followed by the World Cup and another European Championship in 2012.

Barcelona provided many players to Spain as did Real Madrid, and Spain's rise to World Ranking No. 1 was well deserved. In 2008, Spain began to play the style of football that has brought Barcelona 21st Century success. A Fernando Torres goal in 33 minutes was sufficient to beat Germany in Vienna, but four years later, the win was much more emphatic, 4 – 0 over Italy in Kiev with goals from David Silva and Jordi Alba in the first half and Torres and Juan Mata in the second.

PSG & Qatar

Qatar Sports Investments was established in 2005 by the son of the Emir and heir to the Qatari throne, Sheikh Tamim Bin Hamad Al Thani and its most startling investment to date has been its involvement in Paris Saint-Germain (PSG). Initially it bought 70% of the club in 2011 and former Inter Milan coach Leonardo was installed as general manager.

The money available as a result cannot be matched by any other French club and few in world soccer. Before the investment, PSG had no won Ligue 1 since 1994. Subsequently, any season that it did not win was regarded as a surprise. That actually happened in 2016/7 with Monaco winning the title, but at the end of the season, Monaco lost a number of its side to richer clubs, including PSG, so normal service should be resumed.

Just as London appeals to many foreign stars, Paris is attractive to that same group, so recruitment was never going to be a problem. Likewise, it is a huge city with no other clubs competing for the market and the local youth talent. All the ingredients for success were and still are there.

PSG run of four successive Ligue 1 titles began in 2012 – 3 and was only interrupted by Monaco, surely on a temporary basis? The next challenge of course is the Champions League where, as of the 2016/7 season, it has yet to reach the final, never mind win it. The real statement of intent that the Champions League is a real possibility was the world record transfer into PSG of Brazilian, Neymar, which is thought to be for around £200m.

Lionel Messi

Argentinian Lionel Messi was so small as a boy that he needed a growth hormone. That was paid for by Barcelona, whom he joined when he was still very young. Messi has repaid the club many times over with Champions League, La Liga, and Copa del Rey successes throughout his career. He has four Champions League wins, eight La Liga, and five Copa del Rey by the end of 2016/7.

Messi is just 5ft 7 ins., but he has excellent close control and is able to ride tackles. He became only the second player to win the Ballon D'Or three years in a row and has five titles in all. He made his debut for Argentina when he was a teenager and has subsequently played in three World Cups before an anticipated fourth in Russia. It is a trophy he has yet to win, and he has also been disappointed in his efforts to take Argentina to the South American title.

Debate has raged about whether Messi has been the best player ever. He clearly has rivals, including another one currently playing, Cristiano Ronaldo. Messi does appear to be the more complete player within a team, and there is no doubt that Barcelona would not swap him for anyone. His goal scoring record is excellent, but he is also a great creator for others. His 61 international goals have come in 123 appearances while he has now become the highest goal scorer in the history of La Liga. In 612 appearances for Barcelona, he has 530 goals and 240 assists with 366 of those goals in La Liga. He will pass 100 goals in the Champions League sooner rather than later.

Barcelona

The Nou Camp in Barcelona is a great place to watch soccer. Its capacity is currently just below 100,000, making it the largest soccer stadium in Europe. The audience has seen some great games there in recent years. Messi has been central to much of it, but it is important to remember that players like Xavi, Iniesta, and Pique are quality internationals in a Spanish side which has won European and World titles.

Barcelona has won the Champions League four times and La Liga eight times in the 21st Century, not to mention sundry Cup triumphs. The first of those La Liga winners was in 2004/5 and every year since, except 2007/8, there has been a trophy of some kind.

Barcelona and Real Madrid are major rivals with the added factor of the former being in Catalonia, a fiercely proud region in Spain where Real is perceived as the capital's favorite. With Messi still only 30 at the end of the 2016/7 season, it seems likely that Barcelona can expect him to be part of a successful Barcelona side for a few years to come.

FIFA Scandals

FIFA has been the body organizing and controlling the world game for as long as anyone can remember. Its membership has grown steadily from the end of the Second World War with the most discernible difference being the number of African and Asian associations joining up. Where once Europe was all-powerful, that is no longer the case. Joao Havelange from Brazil became President in 1974 with plenty of support from the relatively new members and during his tenure FIFA developed into a global organization with access to huge funds from television and sponsorship. The World Cup saw new destinations and the value for winning the bidding was enormous. Unfortunately, wherever there are huge sums of money involved, there is temptation and corruption.

Not only have there been a number of court cases relating to corruption, the FIFA President for all of the 21st Century, Sepp Blatter, has been removed, quickly followed by the UEFA President Michel Platini, who previously had been seen as Blatter's natural successor.

Stories continue to emerge about decisions made in the past, and there is a great deal of suspicion about lobbying going beyond legal boundaries. There have been a number of decisions called into question, and they include the success of bidding for the World Cup, Germany and South Africa, never mind the single announcement of two future venues, Russia and Qatar, in 2018 and 2022.

Russia & Qatar

In 2010, two new venues for the World Cup were announced at the same time, Russia in 2018 and Qatar four years later.

Sepp Blatter made the announcement in Zurich. He thanked all the bidders for their efforts, and there was a good deal of dejection in the hall.

Vladimir Putin did not attend; he had always been confident of success, and back in 2010, the rumblings about activity behind the scenes were only in the early stages. Two of the FIFA executive from the total of twenty-four were absent, already under investigation but not related to the new World Cup decisions. The other bids had come from England and joint

Spain/Portugal and Belgium/Netherlands with Europe already the chosen continent.

The choice of Qatar was certainly contentious and still is. Temperatures by day in this Gulf State at the time of year when the World Cup is traditionally held are far too hot for playing football and even for supporters to watch and travel around extensively. The answer Qatar offered was that it would build stadia that were air-conditioned with temperatures of 27C promised, solar-powered and carbon neutral.

That promise came off the table soon after the bid was accepted. FIFA's officialdom seemed unconcerned about that because the Cup could be moved to wintertime, in the middle of the European season. Europe used to be the powerhouse of world soccer, both in quality and income generated, but it could be easily outvoted, even as a solid block, by the number of votes from smaller continents. The building programme in Qatar also came under scrutiny for aspects, especially the labor conditions for workers coming into Qatar purely to work on construction sites.

The Russian Competition is imminent at the time of writing, and the group draws have taken place. Whether the Qatar decision is re-examined is questionable, and probably it will not be changed, but there are still questions to be answered.

Cristiano Ronaldo

Ronaldo hails from Madeira and has become more famous that the fortified wine that the island produces. He began his club career on the Portuguese mainland at Sporting Lisbon as a 17-year-old, moving on to Manchester United for £12m while still a teenager and with only a handful of league appearances to his name. He played 196 games in the Premiership scoring 84 goals in all, with a further 95 other games, 34 goals, and a Champions League winners medal and three Premierships. He stayed at United until July 2009 before moving to Real Madrid for in excess of £80m, a record at the time.

At Real Madrid, he was won the Champions League three more times as well as La Liga twice. His record in La Liga is more than a goal a game with his overall record at Real being 422 goals in 418 games. In addition, he has scored 79 international goals in 147 games with Portugal winning Euro 2016 albeit with Ronaldo standing on the touchline.

He matched Messi's record of five Ballon D'Ors with his second successive win in 2017.

Real Madrid Again

Real Madrid's European titles have come in three spurts. There was the first five when the competition was launched and a sixth soon afterwards, three around the Millennium, and a further three recently, including wins in 2015/6 and 2016/7. The first of the three was in 2013/4 when Real faced its city neighbors Atletico in Lisbon. As the game moved towards 90 minutes, Atletico led 1 – 0 with a goal from Godin scored after 36 minutes. Three minutes into injury time, Sergio Ramos leveled the scores, and Real took control. It scored three times in injury time through Gareth Bale, Marcelo, and a 120th-minute penalty from Ronaldo.

Barcelona won the following season, but Real then came back to take the next two titles. Atletico was the opposition again in 2015/6 with the final being held in the San Siro in Milan. This time, the game went a stage further, penalties. The score of 1 – 1 from goals by Sergio Ramos again with Yannick Carrasco equalizing after Antoinne Greizmann had missed a penalty. Real won the shootout 5 – 3.

No club had ever retained the Champions League until Real did so in 2016/7 with an ultimately easy win over Juventus in Cardiff. Juventus had two previous European successes but had lost in finals six times, including the last four between 1996/7 until the previous season. Ronaldo put Real Madrid ahead, but Juve equalized shortly afterwards via Mandzukic. With scores level at the break and no side dominating, it was anyone's match, but Real scored three times without reply in the second period; Casimero (61), Ronaldo (64), Asensio (90).

The Growth in Premiership Revenue

The revenue being generated by soccer in Europe, particularly in England, has been rising dramatically in the 21st Century. For example, when the Premier League was launched in the early 1990s, it was because it was seen as an ideal vehicle for television. The initial television rights were sold for 191m in 1992 on a deal to run for five years.

The figures, all in Sterling (£) for the subsequent deals speak for themselves:

1997 – 2001	670m
2001 – 4	1200m
2004 – 7	1024m, a reduction but not a trend that continued.
2007 – 10	1706m
2010 – 13	1773m
2013 – 16	3018m
2016 – 19	5136m

The implications of a single country's top division being able to justify such figures and increases are widespread. It would only be possible if the viewing numbers justified it. Clearly, it demonstrated that there was a huge worldwide audience for the product which in itself attracted sponsorship and investment.

The problem is that no other league, European or otherwise, generates remotely a comparable amount, making the top English clubs cash rich and therefore attractive to the top players and agents. That is something that has concerned other national associations as well as some of the previous European elite who cannot possibly compete on transfer fees or wages without significant non-soccer-related income.

The current record of English clubs in Europe over the last decade or two is yet to reflect that revenue. Since the Premiership began, Manchester United has two Champion League titles and Chelsea one, which suffers in comparison to Spanish Giants, Barcelona and Real Madrid with four and six, respectively. To an extent, that is partly due to two outstanding talents, Lionel Messi and Cristiano Ronaldo, but whether these two clubs can withstand the pressure on them once those two retire remains to be seen.

Fair Play

Michel Platini's idea of "fair play" was intended to ensure that every club was run prudently. To say that the system in place is flawed understates the current position because how can any club possibly pay £200m for a single player? In addition, the reality is that in many of the smaller European countries, it has created a new elite because of the rewards that the Champions League offers, reward enough to guarantee that a league champion has an excellent chance of retaining its title.

The aim to improve the overall health of club soccer in Europe is admirable of course, and the "legislation" was introduced in

2010 with clubs subsequently subject to scrutiny on their spending. From 2013 onwards, it has been a requirement to allow an independent Club Financial Control Body (CFCB) to analyze the financial figures of all clubs in UEFA competitions.

There are sanctions in place for non-compliance, though they vary from a warning to withholding competition revenue and registration of players for UEFA competitions. In some circumstances, there is even a suggestion of withholding a title. These are all fine words, but remember some of the huge transfer fees currently being spent. They fly in the face of breaking even or even having a small loss.

Clubs who believed it was possible to merely announce sponsorship deals for huge amounts of money found that UEFA wanted to look at the relationship between sponsors and clubs to see whether it was merely owners or associates pumping more money in. This is where the "ice is thin." It required an assessment of whether a sponsorship was far higher than what was regarded as market value.

To date, nothing has been challenged by UEFA or club to any extent, but there is a feeling that UEFA is trying to avoid confrontation with the top European clubs. After all, it has granted the wish of those clubs for the major leagues, five of them—England, France, Germany, Spain, and Italy—to have four guaranteed Champions League spots while downgrading the status for some countries so that their champions have to go through qualifying.

That may partly be to avoid any discussions of a breakaway. In recent years, the two Milan clubs have found it increasingly difficult to qualify for the Champions League, and they still have a presence at the top table of European Club Soccer in the form of the European Club Association which replaced the G14 group nearly a decade ago.

Of equal concern is the establishment of new elites in smaller nations, and to date few at UEFA have commented on the desirability or otherwise of that.

What the Future Holds

These days, there is as much activity going on off the pitch as there is on it. That said, there is now a host of competition at continental and world level, both age group and women, as well as all the traditional competitions that began all those years ago.

There is no doubting the game's popularity manifesting itself in the value of television and sponsorship deals and the worldwide audience that soccer is attracting, especially in the case of club soccer, the English Premiership. Ironically, in terms of attendances at games, the figures for season 2016/7 show that more people watched the second tier of English football, the Championship, than any other league in Europe except the Premiership and the Bundesliga. To beat La Liga is very surprising.

Finance is undoubtedly causing great debate. A club that prides itself on membership of the Premiership must be careful to balance its ambition with its finances. There is an elite at the top of the Premiership that has the resources to pay transfer fees and wages far ahead of the majority of the League. That may be creating an unfair playing field some claim, but it is what it is.

Television is now able to dictate when fixtures are played, and that takes little account of the needs of fans, especially those who want to travel to away matches. Scheduled kick-off times of mid-afternoon on Saturday no longer apply to half the games in top leagues. Late evening kick-offs are aimed at achieving peak viewing figures. The difficulties for away fans are obvious, yet the clubs they support are richly rewarded for their sacrifice.

Agents are now playing an important role in soccer. Successful ones can command huge fees as a percentage of the transfer price, and that seems to be money that the ordinary supporter would rather see invested back into the game. Certainly, players on huge salaries do require professional advice, but you have to wonder whether a tax adviser and a legal adviser could do the job just as well as a fast talker.

Talk of a European Super League rarely makes the front pages of late. In terms of the top Premiership sides, and probably the two Spanish giants, they have little need. After all, their current revenues are good, and a Super League could potentially take away one of their tiers of income stream.

Outside Europe, ambitions are generally realistic. The money in

Europe will continue to attract stars from other parts of the world, especially South America and Africa. South American football remains highly competitive but not as strong as in Europe. Although it is not a competition that gets credence everywhere, the meeting of champion clubs from different parts of the world to get an unofficial world champion more often than not has a European winner.

The African National Champions have varied over the years, which is a good sign. There has been an increasing number of African players making their name in the top European sides since the days of George Weah. African players are always released back to their countries for the Nations Competition that usually takes place in January.

The Chinese League has recently begun to offer huge salaries, though to date, most of the players heading east have been towards the end of their careers. Recently, the Chinese government has signaled that it is unhappy with the flow of money leaving China into soccer, and this may well be reflected in any future deals. Certainly, European clubs, especially again in England, have become attractive to foreign investors, and the majority of Premiership clubs and a fair number of Championship clubs are now foreign-owned.

The USA now has a flourishing soccer league that has attracted players from abroad to supplement the local talent. The failure of the USA to qualify for the 2018 World Cup was certainly a blow, but the future looks brighter. David Beckham, who spent a successful time at LA Galaxy, has plans to open a new franchise in Florida to add to the existing teams, and that is certainly a positive because of Beckham's fame in the world game.

In Australasia, soccer is unlikely to attract the regular crowds of other more established sports. New Zealand failed to qualify for Russia, but the number of locals playing soccer now more than matches those playing rugby, if they don't quite have the same quality. Australia is going to Russia however.

There seems little to challenge soccer as the most popular sport on the planet in terms of participation and spectating. It has come a long way over a century and a half. The days when an outstanding footballer like Wilf Mannion would have to stand on a train on the way to play a game have long gone.

FACTS & FIGURES

1. Greece has made little impact in World Cup soccer and had not played in the European Competition since 1980 when it went to Portugal in 2004 and beat the hosts 1 – 0 in the Final.

2. Leicester City's success in the English Premiership in 2015/6 was astonishing in the days of super team finance. It had nearly been relegated the previous season, but then as Champions, Leicester reached the quarter finals of the Champions League, only losing narrowly to Atletico Madrid over two legs.

3. One of the most recent shocks in the FA Cup was Wigan's FA Cup win in 2013 over Manchester City with a late goal by Ben Watson.

4. Jose Mourinho to date has won the Champions League twice with two of the least fancied teams he has managed, Porto and Inter Milan. He could not win it during his two spells with Chelsea, nor at Real Madrid. His hopes of winning it with an English side now rests with his tenure at Manchester United. To date, he has however won League titles in four countries—Portugal, England, Italy, and Spain.

5. The first all English Champions League Final took place in

Moscow in 2008 between Manchester United and Chelsea. Skipper John Terry slipped as he took his penalty in the shootout, and it was easily saved. If he had scored, Chelsea would have been champions, but as it was, United took the Cup. Chelsea won the Cup in 2012, beating Bayern Munich on its own ground; Terry missed the game through suspension.

6. Portugal's European success in France at Euro 2016 was earned while its captain and star player watched injured from the touchline. The only goal was scored in injury time by Eder.

7. Germany's 7 – 1 defeat of Brazil in the semi-final of the 2014 World Cup in Brazil ranked as one of the most on-sided internationals ever played by top international sides competing against each other. Germany went on to win the Cup once again.

8. When Real Madrid played Atletico Madrid in the 2014 Champions League Final in Lisbon, it was the first time that clubs from the same city contested the final.

9. The UEFA Women's Cup pitted the best Women's club sides together with the first games taking place in 2001. It was subsequently renamed as the Women's Champions League in line with the male competition.

10. Zlatan Ibrahimović, the Swedish striker, has had an

impressive career, including scoring all four goals in a defeat of England. He has won many trophies including league titles in England, Italy, France, the Netherlands, and Spain, and the Europa League with Manchester United; he has never won the Champions League, however.

11. In 2007/8, Derby County was relegated from the Premier League with the fewest points since the win became 3 points; 11 points was the season's total. Its only win was against Newcastle United with the other points coming from eight draws.

12. The domination of two men, Lionel Messi and Cristiano Ronaldo, with five Ballon D'Ors each is without precedent in the history of soccer.

13. Steve Gerrard, the former England captain, had an outstanding career with his only club, Liverpool, winning the Champions League in 2005, but he never won the Premier League. His slip at Anfield against Chelsea, leading to a Demba Ba goal and ultimately a 2 – 0 defeat, was the pivotal moment in the 2013/4 season as Manchester City ultimately overtook Liverpool to win the title.

14. Frank Lampard was Gerrard's regular companion in the England side. His record of 211 goals over 13 seasons with Chelsea was astonishing for a midfield player.

15. The Chinese Super League has started to compete with

Europe's rich clubs for the best talent. Most of those taking up contracts have been towards the end of their careers, but time will tell whether that changes.

16. While Middle East soccer clubs have not been able to create an international presence, investors placing their money elsewhere, such as at Paris St. Germain and Manchester City, are certainly having an impact on world soccer.

17. Celtic went through the entire Scottish domestic season undefeated in 2016/7, winning the treble for the fourth time in its history. There has been little to challenge Celtic since the financial problems of close city rivals Rangers a few years ago.

18. Wales reached the semi-finals of Euro 2016, defeating Belgium along the way, but just fell short in its attempts to reach only its second-ever World Cup Finals in Russia; the only other Welsh appearance in the Finals was in 1958, sixty years ago.

19. Iceland's national population is only the size of a single small English City, yet Iceland was able to eliminate England, beating it 2 – 1 at Euro 2016 with two goals England goalkeeper, Joe Hart, would happily forget.

20. In Turkey, a club puts a star on its shirt for every five championships it wins. Besiktas won the Turkish Super Lig for the second year in a row in 2016/7 and were then able to add a third star for reaching fifteen titles in its history

TRIVIA QUESTIONS

1. Real Madrid has now won twelve Champions League titles. Who did it beat to win is 12th title?

   A   Barcelona

   B   Atletico Madrid

   C   Bayern Munich

   D   Chelsea

   E   Juventus

2. Who missed the crucial shootout penalty for AC Milan meaning Liverpool took its 5th Champions League title?

   A   Andriy Shevchenko

   B   Paolo Maldini

   C   Hernan Crespo

   D   Andrea Pirlo

   E   Kaka

3. Who scored the Chelsea equalizer in real time in 2012 European Cup Final and then the decisive penalty in the shootout?

   A   Fernando Torres

   B   Frank Lampard

   C   Juan Mata

D   Didier Drogba

E   David Luiz

4. Who scored the last second goal that clinched Manchester City's first Premiership title?

    A   Yaya Toure

    B   Sergio Aguero

    C   Vincent Kompany

    D   David Silva

    E   Joe Hart

5. Lionel Messi is a one-club soccer player. What is that club?

    A Real Madrid

    B Chelsea

    C Barcelona

    D Manchester United

    E Juventus

ANSWERS

1. E
2. A
3. D
4. B
5. C

DON'T FORGET YOUR FREE BOOKS

GET THEM FOR FREE ON WWW.TRIVIABILL.COM

MORE BOOKS BY BILL O'NEILL

I hope you enjoyed this book and learned something new. Please feel free to check out some of my previous books on **Amazon**.

Made in the USA
Middletown, DE
06 August 2020